CRA AT FORTY

VIEWS ON THE PRESENT AND FUTURE
OF COMMUNITY REINVESTMENT

CRA AT FORTY: Views on the Present and Future of Community Reinvestment

Editor:
findCRA
235 South Fifth Street, Fourth Floor
Louisville, KY 40202

TABLE OF CONTENTS

CRA AT FORTY: WHERE WE ARE

CRA AT FORTY: WHERE WE'RE GOING

INTRODUCTION

Ben Loehle
findCRA

During the 1950s, the term *inner city* became synonymous with poverty in America – a convenient euphemism for the run-down, older neighborhoods being left behind in the race toward suburban glory. By the early 1960s, it was clear that much more had been left behind than physical places. Entire communities of urban residents had become systematically cut off from goods and services, government support, adequate education, jobs and even homeownership. Crime soared; greater social ills, including riots, came to characterize these neighborhoods. As middle- and working-class families fled en masse over the following decades, the poor and elderly were left to inherit the inner city slums.

With myriad social and economic factors at play, large-scale discrimination was a key contributor to the undoing of American inner cities. Discriminatory lending practices by many banks essentially barred lower-income individuals, the majority African American, from purchasing a home. Public policies that shifted government investment from urban development into suburban development and U.S. Interstate construction demolished low-income neighborhoods and isolated displaced residents.

But not all was lost. The poor, inadequate conditions of one inner city school on the West Side of Chicago eventually spurred Gale Cincotta, a concerned mother, to take action and ignite a movement that would be the beginning of the end of these discriminatory practices and policies.

In the early 1960s, Gale joined the PTA at her sons' school and began pushing for improved conditions not only there, but also in schools throughout the city. By the mid-1960s, she had expanded her activism to push for fairer financial practices among landlords. Armed with a brazen style and deep passion for her community, Cincotta's efforts sparked a string of events that would become one of the greatest grassroots movements in modern American history, culminating in the passage of the Home Mortgage Disclosure Act (HMDA) in 1975 and the Community Reinvestment Act (CRA) in 1977.[1] For banks, the combined impact of these two federal laws meant that they now had to meet the credit needs of individuals throughout their entire market areas and could no longer target only the wealthier neighborhoods.

Today, the CRA continues to be an important tool for combatting the poverty and other social ills that emerged in the 50s and 60s. With several amendments over the years and the rise of an entire *community development* industry, the story of CRA and its impact on America's inner cities is still unfolding. Banks are now obligated to not only offer loans, but also investments and services

---

[1] Michael Westgate and Ann Vick-Westgate, <u>Gale Force—Gale Cincotta: The Battles for Disclosure and Community Reinvestment</u>, March 2011, available at https://www.amazon.com/Gale-Force-Gale-Cincotta-Disclosure-Reinvestment/dp/0615449018

within low-income communities in their markets. A vast array of different types of nonprofit organizations also play a crucial role in helping to meet community needs, from job training and financial literacy to affordable housing financing and homeless shelters.

As the "Mother of CRA," Gale Cincotta would be proud of the progress we've made. A recent study revealed that over a 15 year period, lenders committed almost $4.5 trillion in CRA loans[2], and the annual dollar amount of community development loans is rising. Between 1996 and 2014, total community development loans from banks more than quadrupled, from $17.7 billion to $74.6 billion, respectively.[3] Some of America's bleakest, most forsaken communities have been transformed and revitalized. Yet the underlying forces of poverty remain intact. While many of the historical problems that the CRA sought to remedy, such as discriminatory lending (or "redlining") and government divestment in urban areas, have been and continue to be addressed, many of the core social issues at the root of the problems, including institutionalized discrimination, continue to evolve and threaten our most vulnerable populations and places.

If 40 years of CRA has taught us one thing, it's that community development work is never finished. To be sure, poverty and inequality are some of humanity's oldest, most complex problems. Each new generation brings a new set of trends and issues that not only change *what* poverty and inequality look like, but also *how* they happen. Naturally, these new patterns challenge us to re-affirm our beliefs on what is right and wrong and re-think how we go about doing what is right. As we forge ever-further into an era

---

[2] National Community Reinvestment Coalition, "CRA Commitments," September 2007, available at https://docs.google.com/viewerng/viewer?url=http://community-wealth.org/sites/clone.community-wealth.org/files/downloads/report-silver-brown.pdf

[3] National Community Reinvestment Coalition, "The Community Reinvestment Act: Vital for Neighborhoods, the Country, and the Economy," June 2016, available at http://www.ncrc.org/images/ncrc_cra_affirmation_final.pdf

of rapid change, it's time to address this challenge head-on, to create a brighter future for all of America's communities.

Our ability to shape this future rests on two things: understanding where we are, and communicating the vision for where we want to be. We need to start by going beyond the current headlines, policies and data, and get to the heart and soul of the work. This book tells the stories of community development, from the perspective of those working in our communities, who, like Gale Cincotta, bring their knowledge and passion to bear every day in confronting the most critical problems facing communities in need. While many of the other works on this subject focus on policy and academic research, this is a book about real-world experiences told in plain language, by those who live them. As we pause to reflect on the 40th anniversary of CRA's enactment, their stories and insights provide a lens for us to see CRA at work, ideas for its future and most importantly, what it means in people's lives.

This book is divided into two sections: "Where We Are" and "Where We're Going." Each section features essays from a wide range of professionals, including bankers, consultants, developers, entrepreneurs, nonprofit professionals and policymakers. Their essays incorporate personal stories, observations, facts, statistics, insights and opinions. Individually, each essay provides a snapshot of a particular issue or strategy; collectively, they tell the story of where CRA is today and where it's going into the future.

The first section dives into the current landscape of community development, highlighting the core issues that CRA seeks to address and the impact and challenges of today's most common strategies and practices. From stories of a child's first encounter with poverty to critical assessments of our current practices and regulations, these essays offer an honest, unflinching assessment of where CRA work stands, and what it will need in order to move into the future.

The second half of the book includes essays which look toward that future and put the spotlight on emerging social issues as well as ideas to modernize aspects of the CRA itself and meet community needs through innovative solutions. Collectively, the essays in this section – on topics ranging from the future of affordable housing to flexible credit practices to new, technology-driven modes of giving – make the case for broadening the reach of CRA activities, in terms of what qualifies, who must comply and how much support is provided. They also make the case for a more progressive approach to community development – one that incorporates manufactured housing, overall community health, technology and improved collaboration among all community stakeholders.

Over the past 40 years, the number of Americans living in poverty has increased by nearly 18 million people.[4] Poverty is very much a moving target, and it may seem that even with our best efforts, addressing community needs can be difficult. By reflecting on the stories in this collection, we can shift our focus to the problems and solutions that matter. Doing so not only empowers us to envision the future we want to create, but also share it with those who can make it happen.

This book is dedicated to all those who are affected by poverty and the community development professionals working to meet their needs. I'd like to thank them for having the courage and perseverance to make America a better place to live and work. I want to especially thank all the contributors to this collection, whose stories create an invaluable resource for understanding where CRA stands today and how we can use it to create a better future.

---

[4] Bernadette D. Proctor, Jessica L. Semega and Melissa A. Kollar, "Income and Poverty in the United States: 2015," United States Census Bureau, U.S. Department of Commerce Economics and Statistics Administration, September 2016, available at
https://www.census.gov/content/dam/Census/library/publications/2016/demo/p60-256.pdf

BEN LOEHLE is the Chief Executive Officer and Co-Founder of findCRA, where he leads the direction and execution of findCRA's vision, primarily through product design and development, as well as strategic partnerships and investments. He also works alongside the findCRA leadership team in managing daily operations and ensuring that users and clients receive the tools and support they need to meet their community development goals. Drawing on a diverse background in banking compliance, legal research and customer development, as well as a passion for innovation, Ben is instrumental in finding new ways to support the efforts of banks and nonprofits as they partner together to improve communities. Ben holds a Bachelor's of Science degree in Economics from the University of Kentucky, as well as a background in law through his studies at Nova Southeastern University's Shepard Broad Law School.

WHY CRA MATTERS: TOWARDS AN EQUAL WORLD

Linda Ruffenach
Real Spirit Media

Every one of us enters this world the same way: naked and crying. We all have the same basic needs: food, water and shelter. All of us want to feel loved. We begin life as essentially the same, but it quickly becomes evident that not all of us will be provided with the same opportunities.

What if the type of life you live was determined solely by the zip code where you were born? What if your zip code was the biggest influencer in determining your education level, your earning potential, your life expectancy and your happiness? Unfortunately, far too often, this is the reality.

My son was born into a desirable zip code in an area of Louisville, Kentucky commonly referred to as the Highlands. It's an eclectic neighborhood with older restored homes, a bustling retail strip, restaurants, coffee shops and record stores. Over the years, it has become one of the preferred places in my city to raise young families, offering housing for a wide array of incomes, top-notch options for both public and private schools and access to many parks and recreational spots that support a healthy lifestyle.

From an early age, it was clear that my son sees the world in a particular way. For him, many things are either right or wrong, black or white, fair or unfair. Even as a young child, he was incredibly empathetic to others' pain, and his conflicts were often driven by his staunch belief that everyone should be treated the same.

When he was 10 years old, our family worked together during the holidays to collect items for a daycare across town. My son went with me to deliver the boxes of toys, books, diapers and other necessities. When we pulled up to the daycare, which was situated across the street from a city park, my son noted how different things looked. What he saw in the park were not kids playing but an array of characters doing their business, including a few "pharmaceutical" deals. He noted that the houses and buildings were in need of repair and expressed his level of discomfort as we began to unpack the items in our car.

We went inside and shared our bounty with the site director who then offered to take us on a tour of the facility. We walked around and met the kids, who ranged in age from just a few weeks old to five years. My son interacted with the other kids, asking what they were working on or if they were excited about Santa coming.

On the ride home, my son was particularly quiet. I asked him what was on his mind and he responded with a level of insight that most adults would miss, let alone a 10-year-old.

He was worried about the kids that he met that day. Not because they were not well taken care of, but because even he could see that they were situated right in the middle of a difficult neighborhood, unlike the one where he had grown up. He noted that many of the kids were a lot like him or reminded him of his brother. He wagered that they probably wanted to play in the park across the street but may not have felt safe doing so. He keenly observed the level of security to get in and out of the daycare itself. He thought that it must be tough growing up in an area with such high crime rates and then asked the question, "Mom, how did it get so bad down here? It doesn't seem fair that their neighborhood looks so different from ours. What is their future going to be like?"

That's the question we continually grapple with as we look at the past and future of community reinvestment and the profound opportunities it creates to put resources directly bank into communities. Through these efforts, we can empower real and lasting change that will determine outcomes for neighborhoods, businesses, families and children. What will their future be like – and how will we make sure it's the future we want?

LINDA RUFFENACH is a customer experience guru, original Whisky Chick, crazy good with numbers and spreadsheets and has honed her skills as CEO, therapist and individual brand builder. As the founder of Real Spirit Media, an experimental marketing agency, she is obsessed with crafting and sharing brand stories. She revels in creating experiences that turn into memorable moments, transforming customers into brand ambassadors - each choosing to experience your story repeatedly, telling their friends, families and social networks about who you are and what you do. Linda is also the founder of Whisky Chicks, a social group that specializes in creating events for women, and a few men, to discover and learn about Bourbon and whisky.

CRA AT FORTY

WHERE WE ARE

AMPLIFYING CONNECTION: THE CRA & FAIR LENDING COLLOQUIUM

MARGARET WEIR, ESQ., CRCM
Attorney at Law

Every year, people in the United States look forward to fall: football, pumpkin-spiced everything, fairs, crisp air and decorative gourds galore. Those whose professional role touches on the regulatory compliance areas of the Community Reinvestment Act or fair lending also anxiously await the opportunity to sip their pumpkin spice latte while hearing directly from regulators, industry experts, law and consulting firms and colleagues about specific remedies to shared issues at the Wolters Kluwer **CRA & Fair Lending Colloquium** ("Colloquium").

WHY CRA AND FAIR LENDING?

Why the focus on CRA and fair lending amid an endless sea of competing regulatory priorities? CRA and fair lending affect the root cause of one of our nation's greatest problems: inequality.

Social scientists have created a plethora of research showing that inequality is tied directly to the divide in opportunities to successfully complete higher education. The divide occurs between those families who have, and those that have not, accumulated wealth, and is reflected subsequently in their children's generation.[1] In recent research, Alexandra Killewald of Harvard University points out that it is not just "income inequality" at issue, but rather "wealth inequality" — where wealth determines whether a family can send a child to college and whether the same family has the reserve savings to weather any unplanned, extraordinary expense.[2] The Brookings Institute found that "the share of total wealth owned by the top 0.1 percent increased from 7 percent in late 1970 to 22 percent in 2012."[3] Additionally, "an estimated 35 to 45 percent of wealth is inherited rather than self-made."[4]

---

[1] Matthew Desmond, "How Homeownership Became the Engine of American Inequality," The New York Times Magazine, May 9, 2017, available at https://www.nytimes.com/2017/05/09/magazine/how-homeownership-became-the-engine-of-american-inequality.html

[2] Marc Sollinger, "Innovation Hub: What Inequality Looks Like Right Now," WGBH.com, March 17, 2017, available at http://blogs.wgbh.org/innovation-hub/2017/3/17/berube-killewald-equality/

[3] Isabel V. Sawhill and Edward Rodriguez, "Wealth, Inheritance and Social Mobility," Brookings Social Mobility Memos, January 30, 2015, available at https://www.brookings.edu/blog/social-mobility-memos/2015/01/30/wealth-inheritance-and-social-mobility/.

[4] Ibid.

The best mechanism for ordinary Americans to obtain and grow wealth in the United States is homeownership.[5] This is problematic, since before the CRA and fair lending laws, minorities were often discouraged or excluded from mortgage financial services, or otherwise excluded through redlining practices. Thus, those minority families could not create wealth to pass down. The vicious cycle continues since first-time homebuyers often rely upon familial wealth for a down payment.[6] When that is unavailable, often the only choice is to rent. The cycle of renting makes it virtually impossible to save a down payment without outside assistance, and thus wealth is never created.[7] Inequality is also linked to life satisfaction and happiness.[8] Those individuals who experience perceived income inequality have lower life satisfaction, or "happiness," over the long term, which in turn begets societal discontent.

Access to affordable credit products allows families to purchase homes, thus enabling them to begin to build wealth. Programs such as CRA and fair lending are of paramount importance in bridging the inequalities that engulf race relations today, and affect not only the individuals seeking access to credit, but also our larger society.

Building on these themes, the keynote speaker at the 2015 Colloquium was Vanita Gupta, the principal deputy assistant

---

[5] The Editorial Board, "Homeownership and Wealth Creation," The New York Times, November 29, 2014, available at
https://www.nytimes.com/2014/11/30/opinion/sunday/homeownership-and-wealth-creation.html
[6] Ibid.

[7] Matthew Desmond, "How Homeownership Became the Engine of American Inequality," The New York Times Magazine, May 9, 2017, available at
https://www.nytimes.com/2017/05/09/magazine/how-homeownership-became-the-engine-of-american-inequality.html

[8] Maria Konnikova, America's Surprising Views on Income Inequality, The New Yorker, November 17, 2016, available at https://www.newyorker.com/science/maria-konnikova/americas-surprising-views-on-income-inequality

attorney general and acting head of the Civil Rights Division at the DOJ. She stated that "credit provides a very key rung on the ladder of economic mobility...access to credit enables people to uplift their lives and build a better future" in the American economy. As suggested by the research noted above, she also linked lack of credit as a root cause of civil unrest witnessed in American communities that year (and sadly, since) saying:

> *Underneath so much of the unrest that we've seen...lies a foundation of systemic inequalities and discriminatory biases, built up over decades, not days. To break down the barriers to opportunity, we must protect the rights of people to borrow money without bias or discrimination. Credit provides the means for families to own a home, to buy a car so they can get to work and to increase their earnings so they can invest in their own future.*

Highlighting not only the importance of CRA today, but also the caliber of discussion among participants, one 2016 attendee stated: "CRA is more important now than it has ever been. Low-income people are being redlined and disinvested by forces even more sinister than banks such as private equity, investment banks, technology credit scoring and the overall consolidation of money. It should be extended to all financial services companies."[9]

HONORING INDUSTRY LEADERSHIP

Since 2009, the Colloquium has reserved time during the general session to award The Community Impact Award. The award is intended to encourage groundbreaking community lending and programming, which shows a breadth of positive impact on low- and moderate-income communities. In addition to honoring the person and program that best exemplifies the ideals of innovation

---

[9] Quote by participant, and award honoree, Britt Faircloth, 2016

and service, the award is also useful in providing the financial industry with examples of successful programs.

The 2016 honoree, Britt Faircloth, VP and fair banking manager at Bank of North Carolina, won for the High Point Revitalization Program, which aimed "to revitalize and stabilize blighted or declining neighborhoods while increasing affordable home ownership in those areas." The bank partnered with the city to identify the areas of blight, provided affordable mortgage products to help homebuyers purchase new housing at or near cost and targeted the underbanked and "ignored" parts of the population. The program also featured an educational component for participants: a finance course taken over several months covering essentials such as how to pay property taxes and guidance on insurance and other mortgage elements. In accepting the award, Ms. Faircloth noted, "It was important for [us] to invest in the city where we are headquartered and where we began, as we not only want to improve the areas around us, but also ensure that this community continues to grow."

In 2014, the Colloquium added a second award, named for a practitioner who exhibited passion for data analysis that is inherent in CRA and fair lending compliance: the Alfredo deHaas Excellence in Analytics Award, intended to "trumpet the 'unsung heroes' who creatively and thoughtfully use data to advance their institution's CRA and/or fair lending management goals." The 2016 honoree, Daryl Hall, a compliance officer at Fifth Third Bank in Cincinnati, Ohio, was described by Byna Elliott, SVP and acting director of Community & Economic Development for Fifth Third Bank, as a person who "has a tremendous passion for helping people understand how compliance with the Community Reinvestment Act impacts both our bank and the communities we serve." As this quote illustrates, the data component of CRA and fair lending compliance is not only important for regulatory analysis, but is a useful tool in telling the institution's story to the broader community.

These awards are important recognition for those professionals who are often overworked and underappreciated at their particular institution, but also highlight for a broader public audience the positive impact banks have on communities, in operating in inventive and meaningful ways. Given the number of scandals arising from banks in recent years, it is important to highlight the amazing things banks do to develop and support their communities.

WHAT IS A "COLLOQUIUM" ANYWAY?

The CRA & Fair Lending Colloquium traces its origins back to a "user conference" for a company purchased by Wolters Kluwer, where users of specific CRA and Home Mortgage Disclosure Act ("HMDA") software would convene to engage on best practices, learn about developments and obtain training from company experts. It was clear from feedback received that there was a need for clients to better understand specific CRA and fair lending trends, oversight measures and recent regulatory developments — preferably from experts in the field, and directly from the regulators. With no other industry event available to bridge this gap, the Colloquium was born.

The term "colloquium" is generally considered an academic conference or seminar, where the participating academicians focus on one, very targeted area of study. Thus, the name, "CRA & Fair Lending Colloquium," was chosen to set apart the gathering from other, broader industry conferences. The purpose of this Colloquium is to dive deep into the intricacies of CRA and fair lending. As is the case with academic colloquia, the Colloquium endeavors to create agenda topics and invite esteemed speakers who hold divergent views to serve as catalysts for participants to delve even deeper into the marrow of what it means to have programs that not only meet regulatory scrutiny, but truly serve the original purpose of the organic statutes behind CRA and fair lending — building and sustaining strong communities.

The conference began with barely 100 people gathered in Newport, Rhode Island, a hotel snafu and a thinly stretched staff. The hotel, through either error or low expectations, began to sell rooms set aside for the conference — which forced planners to focus on contract enforcement rather than agenda development for a period of time. Despite these setbacks, the conference staff was able to marshal regulators and other regulatory experts to present a compelling agenda. To hear a veteran of the first session tell the story, it was a harrowing experience behind the scenes. The takeaway was that people were hungry for the information in this targeted, "colloquium" format. The event has blossomed to over 700 participants today.

THE CRA & FAIR LENDING COLLOQUIUM TODAY

The annual Colloquium brings together hundreds of compliance professionals and regulators to discover and discuss regulatory priorities, exam approaches and other firsthand guidance on how practitioners might enhance their institution's CRA and fair lending compliance programs. While there are other general "compliance" conferences that may include agenda items on CRA and fair lending, the Colloquium is the only available setting to bring such a depth of knowledge from all lenses together exclusively on the very important areas of CRA and fair lending. One participant from the 2015 Colloquium put it well in a survey response, stating "so many conferences offer subject matter a mile wide but only an inch deep...whereas the Colloquium really delves deeply on fair lending and CRA issues. I always learn something every year at this conference." This is because the agenda features strategy-oriented sessions focused on emerging trends and issues, not merely a recap of news items and official regulatory actions.

Previous years' sessions have included speakers from leading law and consulting firms, community development, fair housing and consumer advocacy organizations and invaluable participation from major banking regulatory agencies, including the Department of Justice ("DOJ"), the Consumer Financial Protection Bureau ("CFPB"), the Federal Deposit Insurance Corporation ("FDIC"), the Federal Reserve Board ("FRB") and the Office of the Comptroller of the Currency ("OCC").

This is the very best venue for understanding, directly from the source, the current regulatory landscape, including supervisory priorities, as well as providing attendees an unparalleled forum for lively discussion and debate on regulatory developments and concerns. Regulators have indicated that the benefit of being in the same room flows both ways — where the issues faced by practitioners are amplified and receive greater attention than when one banker, or one trade association, makes a case regarding a specific issue. For practitioner participants, the combination of regulators, law firms, consulting firms and colleagues provides a unique opportunity to step away from their institutions and crowd-source CRA and fair lending solutions. Networking among individuals who have a depth of knowledge in this very specialized area is also invaluable, with opportunities to do so built into the schedule each day. Additionally, there are pre-conference, educational "basics" programs for those who may be newer to the field. Finally, there are post-conference Wolters Kluwer user-group focused seminars that allow participants who use Wolters Kluwer systems to manage their CRA and/or fair lending obligations to gain a more in-depth understanding of the capabilities of the systems, and also learn of system updates or any other changes from prior system releases. As a testament to the high quality of programming, several professional certifying organizations offer continuing education credit for Colloquium attendance.

IMPACT OF THE COLLOQUIUM

The full impact of bringing together a hive of so many experts is hard to measure. However, it is clear, through anecdotal evidence, that the Colloquium moves the needle on CRA and fair lending compliance, helping increase one's regulatory quotient. Moreover, it can provide participants the foundations for returning home and challenging themselves to innovate as they have seen others do that were honored for their work in the field. Everyone comes away with best practice ideas that come from all sides of the field, including valuable regulator official input.

Year after year, participants submit rave reviews — previously via surveys, more recently via Twitter and consistently through repeat attendance. Compliance today is complicated, with CRA and HMDA rules changing significantly and requiring more expertise than ever before, across multiple competencies that are not generally bedfellows (data analysis with legal/regulatory analysis, plus program development and management). As the OCC's Grovetta Gardineer tweeted during a 2016 keynote address, "[C]ompliance is not a box to check, it's central to an institution's operations."[10] Going into much more specifics, another participant summarized something he learned on the anonymous survey response: "Perform a regression analysis on [a] large volume of HMDA data consisting of our assessment areas, so that we can more accurately tell our fair lending story. If not, the regulators will tell our story for us. Redlining analysis is crucial. Market share analysis essential." That is information he can take to the bank.

---

[10] Grovetta Gardineer, "Remarks by Grovetta Gardineer, Senior Deputy Comptroller for Compliance and Community Affairs, Before the 2016 CRA and Fair Lending Colloquium, Las Vegas, Nevada, November 15, 2016," available at https://www.occ.treas.gov/news-issuances/speeches/2016/pub-speech-2016-144.pdf

MARGARET "MAGGIE" WEIR, Esq., CRCM, is a regulatory compliance and legal professional with more than 25 years of experience in leadership roles with multiple financial institutions and consulting groups. Maggie is a graduate of the Boston University School of Law where she earned a J.D. and subsequently a LL.M. in Banking and Financial Law. She holds an MBA from the University of Denver and a B.A. in Political Science from the University of Houston. She is a Certified Regulatory Compliance Officer and a graduate of the ABA National Compliance School and Graduate School of Banking at Colorado. She is an attorney in the Boston metro area and serves as adjunct faculty within the J.D. and LL.M. programs at Boston University School of Law. She is also a faculty member for the ABA's National Compliance School and the ABA Graduate School of Compliance Risk Management, as well as a frequent regional and national speaker on relevant legal and business topics.

CRA AND FAIR LENDING: EQUAL PARTNERS

Nancy Presnell & Sheila Etchen
Republic Bank

CRA and Fair Lending – how do we ever tell them apart? Well, for banking compliance officers, the answer is that you better tell them apart, because strict adherence to both regulations is crucial to a positive CRA Performance evaluation. "It is?" you ask. The answer is a resounding: "Yes!"

Of all the changes in the Community Reinvestment Act (CRA) since its beginning in 1977, recent strategies to enforce anti-discrimination by tying the Equal Credit Opportunity Act (ECOA) and the Fair Housing Act to CRA are the most compelling. No change in Interagency Q&A guidance has the impact of downgrading a CRA Performance Evaluation, but a poor Fair Lending review could put on hold a bank's merger or acquisition plans, even though the bank received a "Satisfactory" CRA Rating.

THE GROUND RULES

CRA is <u>all about income</u> – serving low- and moderate-income persons as well as low- and moderate-income neighborhoods. The entire legislation focuses on providing equal levels of service to lower-income persons and neighborhoods by way of loans, investments and services. In other words, CRA is "colorblind;" there is no mention of any personal characteristic, except what percentage of Area Median Income the person or neighborhood falls within.

Fair Lending is <u>all about personal characteristics</u>. Called "protected bases," these all-inclusive characteristics are Race, Color, Religion, National Origin, Sex, Marital Status, Age, Receipt of Public Assistance and Consumer Credit Protection (if the person has in good faith exercised any right under the Consumer Credit Protection Act). As a bank employee, it is illegal to treat people differently based upon these prohibited bases.

Fair Lending related to credit decisions is governed by the ECOA and specifically defines instances where lenders must not discriminate including:

- Varying the terms of credit offered, amount, interest rate, duration or type of loan;
- Using different standards to evaluate collateral;
- Treating a borrower differently in servicing a loan or invoking default remedies; or
- Using different standards for pooling or packaging a loan in the secondary market.

HMDA – THE HOLY GRAIL

A bank's lending performance for both CRA and Fair Lending is measured by a single data source reported in compliance with the Home Mortgage Disclosure Act (HMDA). Regulators take accuracy in HMDA reporting very seriously. Prior to a Fair Lending and CRA Exam, a data validation review is conducted. During this review, an institution is allowed no more than two errors per year on a sample of 40 applications. If the institution's error rate is exceeded, the initial sample is expanded to 60 additional applications and there can be no more than 10 percent overall or 5 percent in any key data field. If this expanded error rate is exceeded, a total scrub of all applications for the period being reviewed must commence. This process can add up to hundreds of staff hours and thousands of overtime dollars.

THE EXAMS

Community Reinvestment

Bank Examiners conduct the CRA Exam on-site at the bank, after reviewing very detailed information provided prior to arriving. During this examination, the examiners are looking at three community development key factors for a large bank – lending, service and investment.

The **Lending** Test counts twice the weight in the overall CRA Ratings. It looks at the home mortgage data including the percent of LMI borrowers; the income level of the location of the loans made by the bank; and innovative or flexible products used to serve LMI populations or areas. It also looks at loans that meet the definition of community development. Small business loans are also reviewed as defined by the revenue size of the business and the income level of the location where the loans were made.

The **Service** Test takes into consideration the bank's retail services, including the bank hours. It evaluates if the bank's locations demonstrate accessibility for low- and moderate-income customers to banking services. It also reviews bank community services that must be "financial in nature" and must meet the definition of community development activities.

The **Investment** Test evaluates bank donations that meet the definition of community development as well as other investments made by the bank that meet the community development definition.

Fair Lending

Once the annual HMDA data is released, examiners analyze and identify institutions that may exhibit a greater risk of fair lending violation. Disparities in applications of the protected bases may exist in pricing, originations, denials or fallout rates. A criteria interview may be held to gather more detail on the bank's application and underwriting practices. If matters remain unresolved, a full file review will be conducted. (This can result in expense in staff time and overtime hours.)

A DYNAMIC STRATEGY

So, what should a bank do to offset risk of a lower CRA Rating because of a poor Fair Lending review? There are three components of a dynamic strategy: Analyze, Communicate and Adjust.

Analyze

Shakespeare wrote "to thine own self be true," and this certainly applies to finding out exactly what is a going on in your organization as it pertains to CRA and Fair Lending performance.

Look hard at the numbers – they tell the story. Start with the current HMDA Disclosure and then keep an in-house quarterly reporting analysis.

Analysis should take two forms: one based upon Income Distribution for CRA monitoring and the other on Personal Characteristics for Fair Lending monitoring. The analyses will be based upon comparisons.

Income Distribution

Analyze what percentage of loans is made to low- and moderate-income applicants and in low- and moderate-income areas. How do the results compare to your peers (other similar-sized financial institutions)? Make sure that you review your bank's lending levels by income for <u>every</u> assessment area. Even assessment areas with just one banking center must show that credit is extended to all income levels.

Don't forget to analyze loans to small businesses. Determine where the businesses are located and which of those loans meet the definition of a small business. Again, compare your bank's performance to your peers.

Personal Characteristics

When conducting your review of personal characteristics of loans for fair lending, analyze:

- The number and percentage of applications taken by Race, Gender, Age and Marital Status of the applicants;
- The number of originations by Race, Gender, Age and Marital Status of the applicants;

- The number and percentage of denials by Race, Gender, Age and Marital Status of the applications; and
- The number and percentage of "fall outs" (withdrawn and incomplete applications) by Race, Gender, Age and Marital Status of the applicants.

Your analysis of lending patterns should be based upon personal characteristics comparisons of those loans made to an opposite groups (e.g., loan originations to applicants over age 62 compared to loan originations to those under age 62).

Take a close look at what you discovered. For example,

- Is lending to low- and moderate-income individuals in some of your bank's assessment areas above your peers, while other assessment areas lag behind?
- What were the denial rates among certain protected classes or ethnic groups? Are they higher than white applicants?
- Are more loans made to male applicants than female applicants?
- Are applicants over age 62 being denied financing more than younger applicants?

Communicate

Once the data is compiled and positive impacts, as well as challenges, to CRA and Fair Lending are noted, the news must be communicated throughout the financial institution to senior management, loan officers, business bankers, underwriters, processors, etc. All have a role in making changes to improve CRA and Fair Lending performance.

First, they have to "know the numbers." This can be accomplished by regular meetings with bank staff at all levels in your institution. Creating and communicating with a senior level CRA and Fair

Lending review group will be a good start, but the momentum can't stop there. It is important to involve all players in the lending process.

Involving staff in finding answers to specific questions raised by the data analysis can be a learning experience for staff, as well as senior management. For example, if a significant percentage of applications "fall out" or are never completed, staff could be assigned to investigate and tabulate the reasons why. This will involve conversations with loan officers and processors. Even if the "fall outs" show no fair lending concerns, the research and results could lead to better file documentation and stronger follow-up with applicants.

Presenting case studies of specific loans for discussion is a powerful tool in communicating facts regarding performance. For example: what if you identify a minority loan applicant who applied for a home mortgage with a low debt-to-income ratio, low loan-to-value on their home and a high credit score, however, the applicant was semi-retired and therefore denied because they did not have a current two-year job history? You could discuss what could have been done to help this applicant. Asking questions like this can lead to greater awareness on the part of your bank staff to "go the extra mile" in reviewing a file or look at policy and procedure adjustments, if necessary.

Adjust

Once analysis of CRA and Fair Lending performance is current and ongoing, and bank staff is briefed, the question arises, "What more can we do to create and maintain commitment to CRA and Fair Lending?" How can change occur in the culture of the bank so that service and inclusion are closely held values?

Several best practices can be implemented:

- Engage all staff in discussions of CRA and Fair Lending responsibilities via lunch time talks or presentations by local community groups;
- Provide bank staff with service opportunities that qualify for CRA credit and address needs of a diverse population;
- Encourage senior management to allow paid service hours for time away from the office to support community projects; or
- Create a matching program for staff donations to philanthropic organizations.

Even though CRA and Fair Lending are very different from a compliance perspective, in today's regulatory environment they must be treated as "equal partners" if a bank is to achieve a positive CRA rating. By knowing the numbers, communicating to staff and working to create an all-staff awareness of the issues, the bank will be in a strong position to achieve not only "satisfactory," but an even higher CRA Rating.

NANCY PRESNELL, Managing Director of Compliance, and SHEILA ETCHEN, CRA Officer, both at Republic Bank of Louisville, Kentucky, have survived countless Fair Lending and CRA examinations. They have learned a thing or two and continue to fight the good fight.

COLLABORATION IS KEY

Corey Aber & Simone Beaty
Freddie Mac

For 40 years, the Community Reinvestment Act has motivated lenders to focus on some of the most persistent housing challenges in their local areas. The needs that led to the establishment of CRA are at least as great now as they were in 1977. Like findCRA, Freddie Mac is committed to supporting lenders' efforts to keep housing affordable in their communities.

For 47 years, in good economic times and bad ones, Freddie Mac has fulfilled our mission to promote liquidity, stability and affordability in the U.S. housing market. Being in the secondary mortgage market, we don't make loans. Rather, we buy loans that meet our standards from approved lenders nationwide; lenders use the money from those sales to make loans to other qualified borrowers. To us, supporting housing affordability is more than a mission – it's in our DNA.

Tackling housing affordability takes cooperation on many levels, from many sectors. The economic crisis disrupted many of the supports and connections that make up the housing ecosystem and promote the flow of business. Understandably, a priority for lenders and other stakeholders – including Freddie Mac – became finding ways to help homeowners keep their homes, where possible, and mitigating losses.

Over the last few years, focus has shifted back to expanding opportunities for affordable housing. Because Freddie Mac touches every part of the ecosystem, we are taking the lead in helping to reenergize it and keep it active. As we build a better housing finance system in general, we're enhancing access to the liquidity and other resources that lenders need to meet CRA objectives and effect positive change in their communities. This includes having the right capabilities in place, promoting outreach and education and reaping the benefits of access to data.

FOCUS ON AFFORDABILITY

A key to providing lenders the support they need is giving them access to people, processes, policies, products and services that will make a difference.

Freddie Mac Multifamily, for example, has long been committed to affordable housing preservation, and we've been steadily and significantly investing in our platform and products for the last decade, envisioning the future of housing finance even in the depths of the crisis. As a result, lenders and investors have gained ways to support affordable housing in their communities and nationwide by making loans and selling them to us, investing in Low-Income Housing Tax Credit (LIHTC) equity on properties for which Freddie Mac is the permanent debt provider and investing in securities backed by affordable housing, thereby increasing their ability to meet CRA objectives.

More specifically, following are some of our industry-leading financing programs that support creating and preserving affordable housing, many of which align with CRA:

- Tax-Exempt Loans (TEL) and Bond Credit Enhancements for properties with 4 percent LIHTC;
- Cash loans for properties with 9 percent LIHTC;
- Cash loans for properties with project-based Section 8;
- Loans for HUD's Rental Assistance Demonstration (RAD) program;
- Small Balance Loans (SBL) that support small properties (five to 50 units); and
- Loans for manufactured home communities.

In addition, these credit-risk transfer mechanisms promote private investment for public good:
- K-Deals, our flagship securitization technology;
- ML-Deals, for securitizing Tax Exempt Loans;
- TEBS, for securitizing pools of Tax Exempt Bonds;
- SB-Deals, for securitizing Small Balance Loans; and
- Participation Certificate Programs.

We continually work to streamline processes and develop products to meet borrowers' range of needs. And our in-house, regionally-focused staff has the expertise and flexibility to craft solutions that benefit all parties, while maintaining loan quality.

Our efforts make a difference: About 90 percent of the units we fund each year are affordable to low- and moderate-income renters. And we've broken purchase-volume records several years in a row.

On the Single-Family side, we've transformed our business, renewing the energy around expanding homeownership – responsibly. Our regionally-focused team works in partnership with lenders of all sizes to understand and address business needs; we've significantly increased support for community lenders. We've also reconnected with housing finance agencies (HFAs) and maintain relationships with housing professionals, not-for-profit housing organizations and community organizations. This uniquely enables us to act as a catalyst within the housing finance system, to create avenues and opportunities to reach more borrowers.

To equip lenders to increase affordable lending, we've streamlined processes, refined policies and enhanced products. For example, we extended our Home Possible® suite of products to allow for down payments as low as 3 percent for first-time and low- and moderate-income buyers as well as other buyers in underserved areas; the suite also includes an offering exclusively for HFAs.

Also, Test and Learn pilots are a way to try out new and enhanced products on a small scale before broader release – especially as we work to meet the evolving needs of current and future homebuyers. We're always looking for ways to increase liquidity where it could do the most good.

An example is our initiative with Next Step Network, Inc., to implement online education for buyers of manufactured homes – an affordable option for many low- and moderate-income households. The program, which findCRA participates in, aims to foster relationships in the manufactured housing industry – including with mortgage lenders – locally and nationally.
Manufactured housing is one of three focus areas that comprise the federally mandated Duty to Serve program, the others being rural housing and affordable housing preservation.

Duty to Serve is a welcome opportunity for Freddie Mac as a whole to expand the scope of support and to guide the mortgage industry in looking at housing issues in new ways, understanding the broader problems facing these markets and developing effective and standardized solutions to some of society's most persistent housing problems. We look forward to giving lenders additional tools and resources for serving communities that need it most. The three-year plan that we expect to execute starting in January 2018 will reflect much-appreciated input from across the industry.

IMPORTANCE OF KNOWLEDGE OF NETWORKS

Other key success factors: Outreach and education.

To help lenders and other housing professionals understand and take full advantage of our products, policies and processes, Freddie Mac holds and otherwise supports numerous educational and networking opportunities each year, reaching thousands across the industry.

Our Single-Family team helps lenders with a CRA focus expand their capacity to meet their goals by enabling greater access to and interaction with potential homebuyers. For example, our CreditSmart® financial-literacy curriculum helps people improve their credit and understand the responsibilities of homeownership. Available in several languages, it can be taught by lenders and not-for-profits; it also can be accessed on FreddieMac.com, along with our blog and My Home by Freddie Mac®, which offer a wealth of consumer information and resources that housing professionals may share with clients.

Our Borrower Help Centers (BHCs), run together with HUD-approved housing counseling agencies, deliver education, such as CreditSmart, and counseling services – especially to those with low and moderate incomes. Launched during the economic crisis in hardest-hit cities to assist struggling borrowers, they've refocused on promoting sustainable homeownership. Our fourteenth BHC opened this year in Mississippi – the first in a rural area. Initially covering three counties, it now serves 11. In the first half of 2017,

BHCs worked with 19,000 potential homebuyers and referred almost 10,000 to lenders.

An initiative that harnesses the power within communities is Block by Block, which aims to revitalize urban neighborhoods still struggling to recover from the crisis. Launched in Chicago's Auburn Gresham neighborhood in 2015, it brings together local public, private and not-for-profit organizations to promote sustainable recovery. Today, fewer homes there are vacant and homeownership is increasing. The initiative expanded to Baltimore last December.

BIG DATA, BIG FUTURE

The importance of data and technology is only increasing, as more processes are handled online and systems are integrated. The real benefit will be the access to data this affords us, and the real value will come from how we use that data.

In Single-Family, for example, Freddie Mac's innovative Loan Advisor Suite® integrates the loan-origination process from end to end. It increases reliability, efficiency and certainty, while lowering the cost of producing high-quality loans, and it bolsters lenders' ability to make more loans using more of our credit box – responsibly. And it captures all mortgage-related data and makes it easy to access, share and analyze.

CONTINUING THE COMMITMENT

Access to affordable, available and appropriate housing remains a serious issue nationwide. Importantly, CRA focuses lenders' attention on addressing those challenges in their local areas. Lenders have Freddie Mac's support, rooted in our commitment to our mission and to serving as a catalyst within the housing finance system. Working together, we can help strengthen communities – responsibly and sustainably.

CORY ABERY leads Freddie Mac Multifamily's Community Mission efforts to reach new markets and communities and support affordable housing and underserved markets nationwide. Mr. Aber has been with Freddie Mac for twelve years. He is a graduate of Brown University, where he studied History, Literature and Architecture History.

SIMONE BEATY is the director of affordable lending strategy and policy for Freddie Mac's Single-Family Business, where she's focused on underserved markets, including rural housing and manufactured housing as well as affordable housing preservation. Simone has 19 years of experience in the mortgage industry and has been with Freddie Mac for 13 years. She was previously director of servicing policy. Simone was instrumental in developing Freddie Mac's policy and implementation of the federal government's Home Affordable Modification Program (HAMP), the Neighborhood Stabilization Initiative and the standardization of servicing requirements under the Servicing Alignment Initiative with the Federal Housing Finance Agency.

FREDDIE MAC makes home possible for millions of families and individuals by providing mortgage capital to lenders. Since our creation by Congress in 1970, we've made housing more accessible and affordable for homebuyers and renters in communities nationwide. We are building a better housing finance system for homebuyers, renters, lenders and taxpayers. Learn more at FreddieMac.com, Twitter @FreddieMac and Freddie Mac's blog FreddieMac.com/blog.

WISE INVESTMENT: DRIVING GREATER SOCIAL IMPACT WHILE MEETING CRA NEEDS

Jessica Botelho
Community Capital Management

Community development has proven to be a viable investment approach for thousands of individual investors, small businesses and large institutions, including some of the nation's most prominent and successful banks.

In fact, for banks, investing in communities is more than just a viable business strategy. The Community Reinvestment Act has long mandated providing access to credit and capital to all credit-worthy borrowers in the community. Congress passed the CRA in 1977, requiring that each federally insured depository institution meet the credit needs of the communities they serve, including low- and moderate-income neighborhoods, without compromising safety and soundness. In 1989, Congress passed the Financial Institutions Reform, Recovery, and Enforcement Act (FIRREA), which introduced a four-tier grading system for measuring a bank's CRA performance and mandated public disclosure of all CRA reviews. And in 1995, the regulatory bodies implemented a new "three-pronged" CRA exam that evaluates depository institutions' performance based on lending, service and investments.

The CRA Qualified Investment Fund, also known as "CRA Shares" (ticker: CRAIX), was launched in 1999 as a vehicle for banks looking to satisfy the "investment" test portion of their CRA exam. Because the CRA does not differentiate between a direct or indirect qualified investment[1], the CRA Fund was created as a vehicle for banks to make CRA-qualified investments while also having the capability to target the exact geographies or communities they want those investments to support. This process, called "earmarking," ensures that qualified investments directly benefit the banks' communities.

Since the inception of the CRA Fund, Community Capital Management (CCM), its registered investment adviser, has taken careful steps to ensure that qualified investments are never "double counted" and are only earmarked on a dollar-for-dollar basis. The CRA Fund's earmarking process is driven by the bank shareholder providing information on its county-level assessment areas ("AAs"). The bank shareholder informs CCM whenever there are any changes to its AAs. Qualified investments in those targeted AAs are then purchased and earmarked dollar-for-dollar to the bank shareholder. The bank shareholder receives extensive documentation to support that the primary purpose of each investment is "community development." This process repeats itself based on each bank's CRA exam schedule.

---

[1] *Interagency Questions & Answers Regarding Community Reinvestment,* July 25, 2016 Q&A__.23(a)-1

All the CRA Fund's investments finance a variety of community development initiatives, helping communities in ways that go beyond the straightforward benefits we see on paper. Additionally, many have won awards for excellence in community and economic development and design. One recent example is an investment financing the Congress Building in CCM's backyard of Miami, Florida. The building is a historic Beaux Arts high-rise community with 128 units for low-income tenants. Originally built in 1923 as office space, it was added to the National Register of Historic Places in 1985 and later restored and converted to affordable apartments in 1998. On-site resident amenities include financial counseling, educational courses and job training. Looking at off-site benefits, the property is conveniently located next to the Miami-Dade Metromover, a free mass transit automated people mover train system with routes to 21 stations throughout the city.

Today, after 18 years of investing in communities, the $2 billion CRA Fund remains a powerful tool for over 400 banks, of all shapes and sizes, looking to satisfy their CRA investment requirements. As a result, CCM's proactive, socially conscious approach to fixed income investing has made a direct, positive impact – nearly $8 billion worth – in underserved communities in all 50 states across America, including inner-city neighborhoods, rural communities and regions devastated by natural disasters. This translates into 383,000 affordable rental units; 16,700 affordable mortgages; $336 million in enterprise development and job creation; $412 million in economic development; $894 million in statewide homeownership and down payment assistance; and $33 million in affordable healthcare and rehabilitation facilities. Beyond the numbers, my colleagues and I have seen firsthand the impact these investments have on communities in ways that are difficult to quantify but easy to qualify. These investments have saved beautiful buildings, improved the neighborhoods they reside in and benefited the people who live in and around them. These investments bring an all-important human element to work that can sometimes feel removed.

What started as a tool for banks to meet their CRA obligation has now grown to include investments from foundations, pension funds, religious organizations, not-for-profits, family offices and many others. As the CRA turns 40 and continues to be an important and significant part of our nation's financial legislation, we are excited to support its ongoing positive impact in our nation's underserved communities.

Community Capital Management is an investment adviser registered with the Securities and Exchange Commission under the Investment Advisers Act of 1940. The CRA Qualified Investment Fund is distributed by SEI Investments Distribution Co. (SIDCo). SIDCo is not affiliated with Community Capital Management. Investing involves risk, including possible loss of principal. Bonds and bond funds are subject to interest rate risk and will decline in value as interest rates rise. The Fund is not diversified.

Carefully consider the Fund's investment objectives, risks, charges, and expenses. This and other information can be found in the Fund's prospectus which can be obtained by calling 866-202-3573. Please read it carefully before investing.

Impact figures are approximate since inception (8/30/99) as of 6/30/17. The Congress Building investment represented 0.28 percent of the Fund's assets as of 6/30/17.

JESSICA BOTELHO is the Director of CRA & Impact Research at Community Capital Management. In this role, she is responsible for overseeing and gathering all impact and CRA research as well as impact investing reporting. She additionally manages all facets of CRA Investment Test needs including CRA documentation and fulfillment, proactive summary earmarking letters prior to a banks' CRA exam and maintaining relationships with federal regulators. Jessica joined CCM from Acadian Asset Management. Jessica received her B.S. in Business Marketing from the University of Massachusetts Dartmouth, Charlton College of Business. She holds FINRA licenses Series 6 and 63.

PRESERVING AMERICA'S AFFORDABLE RENTAL HOUSING: THE CRA CASE

Ellen Lurie Hoffman
The National Housing Trust

Preserving affordable rental housing is critical to addressing America's housing affordability crisis and promoting economic opportunity. Preservation success depends upon policy innovation, mission and low-cost financing. Through the Community Reinvestment Act, banks can play an essential and profitable role in housing preservation.

A GROWING GAP BETWEEN AFFORDABLE HOUSING NEEDS AND SUPPLY

Today, the nation faces a rental housing affordability crisis, as rent levels climb and incomes stagnate. In 2015, 26 percent of all renter households nationwide paid more than 50 percent of their incomes for housing. The lowest-income Americans face the most serious housing challenges. Excluding inadequate and unavailable units, there were only 35 affordable rentals for every 100 extremely low-income renters.[2]

In the United States, a person would have to earn $21.21 per hour and work 40 hours a week for 52 weeks a year to afford the average two-bedroom rent. This national average is almost three times the federal minimum wage.[3] Meanwhile, the loss of affordable multifamily rental units has resulted in fewer eligible households receiving housing assistance. Congressional funding for subsidizing rent for the lowest income families has not kept pace with the need. The number of very low-income renters increased from 18.5 to 19.2 million between 2013 and 2015, but the share receiving assistance declined from 25.7 percent to 24.9 percent.[4]

EXISITING AFFORDABLE HOUSING IS AT RISK

In the context of declining subsidies and rising development costs and private market rents, preserving affordable housing has become more urgent than ever. As the Joint Center for Housing Studies at Harvard University reports, the existing stock of

---

[2] The State of the Nation's Housing 2017, pages 31 and 35, Joint Center for Housing Studies at Harvard University (2017)

[3] Out of Reach 2017, pages 1-2, National Low Income Housing Coalition (2017)

[4] The State of the Nation's Housing 2017, page 35, Joint Center for Housing Studies at Harvard University (2017)

affordable housing is at risk. Between 2015 and 2025, 2.2 million privately owned, federally assisted apartments will lose their affordability restrictions, allowing property owners to convert their units to market rents.[5]

- Apartments subsidized with HUD's project-based rental assistance (PBRA) house over 1.2 million low-income households and are a critical source of affordable housing in many communities. PBRA properties are privately owned, with rents subsidized under federal contracts. Once those contracts expire, property owners can opt out and raise rents. Contracts on more than 380,000 PBRA units will expire over the next decade.[6]

- Nearly 60 percent of the rentals with expiring subsidies are Low-Income Housing Tax Credit (Housing Credit) units. These apartments can be retained as affordable if the property receives other subsidies with affordability restrictions or the owner obtains a new allocation of Housing Credits to fund capital improvements.[7] Units in low-poverty neighborhoods are at higher risk.[8]

- Privately owned, "naturally occurring affordable housing" (NOAH) is increasingly lost to renovations and subsequent rent increases in high-cost areas where demand for affordable housing is strong, but new construction is focused at the upper end of the market.

---

[5] America's Rental Housing: Expanding Options for Diverse and Growing Demand, page 31, Joint Center for Housing Studies at Harvard University (2015)
[6] The State of the Nation's Housing 2017, pages 36, Joint Center for Housing Studies at Harvard University (2017)

[7] America's Rental Housing: Expanding Options for Diverse and Growing Demand, page 32, Joint Center for Housing Studies at Harvard University (2015)

[8] The State of the Nation's Housing 2017, pages 36, Joint Center for Housing Studies at Harvard University (2017)

- The aging of the nation's public housing stock also is a concern, with more than half of the units built before 1970. The capital needs for this stock is a staggering $25 billion. Congress has recently provided funding and mechanisms to privatize this stock.

- There is also a need to preserve small multifamily rental housing. This older rental stock is more likely to be in poor condition.[9]

PRESERVATION IS COST EFFECTIVE

Preservation is the obvious first step to address our nation's rental housing affordability crisis. For every new affordable apartment created, two are lost due to deterioration, abandonment or conversion to more expensive housing. Without preserving existing affordable housing, we fall two steps back for every step forward we take. In distressed neighborhoods, preserving affordable housing can spark the public-private investment needed to catalyze the revitalization of an entire community. Saving decent, affordable housing is also a cost-effective way to protect a critical community asset in rapidly gentrifying communities.

Preservation is significantly less expensive than constructing new affordable housing. Rehabilitating an affordable apartment can cost one-third less than building a new apartment. In more expensive communities with high land costs, the cost of building new affordable housing could be as much as double the cost of preserving existing housing. Preservation projects utilizing Housing Credits required 50 percent less Housing Credit equity per unit than new construction developments.

---

[9] America's Rental Housing: Expanding Options for Diverse and Growing Demand, pages 14-15, Joint Center for Housing Studies at Harvard University (2015)

HOW CAN BANKS SUPPORT AFFORDABLE HOUSING PRESERVATION THROUGH CRA?

Lenders play a critical role in affordable housing preservation, investing in local communities and earning CRA credit. For example:

Sharing in predevelopment financing. The most difficult aspect of pursuing preservation projects occurs in the predevelopment phase. To evaluate the financial feasibility of preservation plans, studies must be completed and professionals must be engaged. Often, nonprofit organizations do not have sufficient capital to engage in such predevelopment work.

Both financial institutions and nonprofit developers benefit if they share in this risk. Banks may agree to provide predevelopment dollars for a project, in exchange for a more substantial and/or longer-term participation in permanent future financing of the project. Lenders' more substantial roles may include direct purchase of tax-exempt bonds or Housing Credits, or provision of construction loans.

Investing in intermediaries such as Community Development Financial Institutions (CDFIs). Community development organizations also raise funds to finance predevelopment and interim development loans at below market rates to local nonprofit developers. Banks provide key investments to capitalize these funds, thereby earning CRA credit.

For example, the National Housing Trust Community Development Fund (NHTCDF) is a flexible source of predevelopment and interim development funds for mission-aligned development organizations working to purchase, rehabilitate and preserve affordable housing. NHTCDF has made over $36 million in loans in 28 states and the District of Columbia to preserve almost 12,000 homes. These loans have leveraged more than $1 billion in private and public financing to fund affordable housing preservation. NHTCDF recently launched a new product for energy retrofits and renewable energy.

Purchasing Housing Credits from state and local housing agencies. As Congress cuts affordable housing resources, rents rise, incomes stagnate and property owners opt to profit from market rate conversions, many states, cities and counties are increasing resources dedicated to affordable housing preservation and development. Nearly all states now prioritize preservation in their competitive Housing Credit Qualified Allocation Plans (QAPs). For instance, Michigan offers both a 25 percent set-aside of Housing Credits exclusively for preservation and points for projects involving the preservation of properties with existing subsidies. In contrast, Oregon offers a substantial amount of points for preservation activities, but no set-aside.

Recently, 48 percent of all Housing Credits allocated were deployed to preservation projects. Many banks purchase Housing Credits, which are used to acquire and renovate existing multifamily housing. The same lender that provides the bridge and take-out financing can acquire a property's Housing Credits. By purchasing Housing Credits from state and local housing agencies, banks can obtain CRA credit and support critical preservation activity. Multi-investor funds, which include community and regional banks as investors, are the investment vehicle of choice for Housing Credits.

Similarly, nearly all state housing trust funds support preservation activities and many funds prioritize them as preferred activities. Some cities and counties also dedicate tax revenues to affordable housing preservation. For more information on state and local preservation policies, visit NHT's preservation catalog at www.prezcat.org.

SUPPORTING ENERGY EFFICIENCY INVESTMENTS

Banks may earn CRA credit for making loans to borrowers to finance renewable energy, energy-efficient or water conservation equipment or projects that support the development, rehabilitation, improvement or maintenance of affordable housing. The cost of energy is the largest operating expense in affordable multifamily housing. Energy efficient improvements enable owners to reduce operating expenses, allowing them to maintain affordable rents, reduce greenhouse gases and provide resident services. Federal financial regulators have recognized that loans enabling energy efficiency measures help reduce the cost of operating or maintaining affordable housing as CRA-eligible community development loans.

Loans to CDFIs that support energy efficiency initiatives should be considered community development loans. The central barrier to making more "green" loans is access to the low cost long-term capital needed to make them work.

Underwriting loans against energy savings requires making loans that fully amortize over 8-15 years. CDFIs generally do not have longer-term capital to support this kind of project. Banks providing long-term financing to support CDFI energy efficiency loans should receive CRA credit.

CONCLUSION

As the nation confronts a rental housing affordability crisis, banks can help safeguard hundreds of thousands of affordable homes that serve as the foundation of vibrant communities while earning CRA credit. Bank resources should be harnessed to protect housing, which is critical to ensuring economic mobility and opportunity to those less fortunate in our society.

ELLEN LURIE HOFFMAN joined the National Housing Trust in May 2014 as the Federal Policy Director. NHT is a national leader in preserving and improving affordable housing, ensuring that privately owned rental housing remains in our affordable housing stock and is sustainable over time. Prior to joining the Trust, Ms. Lurie Hoffman worked for the National Council of State Housing Agencies (NCSHA) for nine years, where she analyzed and advocated for federal multifamily housing policy issues on behalf of the nation's state Housing Finances Agencies (HFAs). Ms. Lurie Hoffman holds a Master in Public Policy degree from Harvard University's John F. Kennedy School of Government and a Bachelor of Arts degree in Political Science from Vassar College.

WHAT CRA MEANS TO ME:

SUPPORTING LIVES AND EMPOWERING COMMUNITIES

Michael Lane
Better Tomorrows

At the heart of the Community Reinvestment Act is affordable housing, and in many of America's major cities and communities, we are experiencing an affordable housing crisis. In addition to this core need for housing, many of the residents of affordable housing developments have significant other social and community needs they are navigating every day.

Better Tomorrows was founded in 2013 as a nonprofit organization with a mission to support low-income housing communities by providing comprehensive programming and individualized case management services that empower children, seniors, families and neighborhoods to thrive. To that end, we provide services to more than 26,000 residents of over 100 low-income housing communities in 19 states. Since its inception,

Better Tomorrows has committed itself to providing our communities with three core areas of services: (1) Academic Engagement; (2) Aging in Place; and (3) Case Management.

OUR APPROACH FOR SUPPORTING LOW-INCOME COMMUNITIES

First, Better Tomorrows provides an on-site Social Service Coordinator for each of its communities. This arrangement enables Better Tomorrows' Social Service Coordinators to develop relationships with their residents, which in turn informs them of their specific needs. Second, Better Tomorrows further addresses our residents' needs through our multi-layered programming, which is held year-round and on-site in each community. As our communities and residents are diverse, so too is the programming which is provided.

For children, we provide Out of School Time (OST) Programming that includes curriculum-based After School and Summer Enrichment. Our OST programming includes STEAM, reading and literacy and Get Active components, such as Soccer for Success, which is an evidence-based program Better Tomorrows delivers in partnership with the U.S. Soccer Foundation. These programs are held throughout the entire year and provide our children with an immersive experience that strives to help them succeed not only in school, but in life as well.

Similarly, programming for adults and seniors has been designed to enrich and empower their lives. Examples of these programs include a healthy lifestyle program that promotes food access, nutritional education and preventative healthcare as well as community engagement. Better Tomorrows' healthy lifestyle program has been enhanced by one of our newest initiatives – creating on-site community gardens. In the past two years, Better Tomorrows has created four gardens: an in-ground garden for a family site; outdoor table gardens for two senior sites; and an indoor aeroponic garden (which uses air rather than soil to grow plants) at another senior site. In addition to providing critical food resources, Better Tomorrows' community gardens also serve as a vehicle for active resident engagement for children, adults and seniors.

Case Management Services are also a critical component of Better Tomorrows' impact. These services, as with all Better Tomorrows programming, are designed to accommodate each community's and individuals' unique needs. To achieve this goal, our on-site Social Services Coordinators work with each community resident to create individualized goals and care plans to ensure that they are connected to the services that they and their families require.

When dealing with a multitude of communities in various geographic locales, one of our most critical needs is capturing and managing resident and program data for each community. In this endeavor, Better Tomorrows has singled itself out as a solid data-driven organization. Utilizing Efforts to Outcome ("ETO") software specifically designed for Better Tomorrows' needs, data is compiled on-site by Better Tomorrows Social Service Coordinators. The data is then analyzed and studied each month and shared with all Better Tomorrows staff. This unique strategy continually informs Better Tomorrows on the strengths and challenges of programs, changing resident needs and the "health" of each of our communities.

One of Better Tomorrows' proudest achievements, in addition to serving our communities, is the strong partnerships and collaborations we have developed. Our Soccer for Success program was developed in partnership with the U.S. Soccer Foundation. Similarly, we developed a strong relationship with AmeriCorps which, in turn, resulted in our being awarded a three year PennSERVE grant for our senior residents in Pennsylvania.

CRA AND BETTER TOMORROWS

At Better Tomorrows, a majority of our programs and services are in direct alignment with the Community Reinvestment Act, starting with the individuals and neighborhoods we support. We are focused on ensuring economic stability for our residents in a variety of ways including job training, subsidized employment, job retention and job enhancement. We also support our residents with safe credit and borrowing education and sound financial planning.

We know that personal and community health play a strong part in revitalizing neighborhoods. We encourage healthy lifestyle choices that provide opportunities for physical activity, healthy eating and prevention of chronic health problems, many of which fall in line with the Federal Reserve's guidance for Healthy Communities. Simultaneously, we support efforts that prevent social problems in low-income neighborhoods including drug and alcohol addiction, violence, abuse and crime. We strive to ensure that our communities are safe and supportive.

EMPOWERING COMMUNITIES

Since our creation, we have served thousands of residents of low-income communities. Our After School Program has supported nearly 1,000 youth, with almost 700 youth participating in our Summer Enrichment Program. We have also distributed over 600,000 pounds of critically needed food. We have partnered with 525 organizations and individuals to support our communities. In 2016, we were honored to be awarded a three-year grant by AmeriCorps/PennSERVE to address social isolation in senior communities in Pennsylvania.

As we approach our fifth anniversary in 2018, Better Tomorrows is excited to take a moment to reflect on our journey, take pride in our accomplishments, learn from our challenges and continue to expand and enhance our vision and commitment to the communities we serve. We are proud of providing our services to these communities that need them most, that are so closely aligned to the same communities that banks support under the CRA. Together, we can all reinvest in making our communities strong, safer and more vibrant for many years to come.

MICHAEL LANE is the Director of Development at Better Tomorrows located in Marlton, New Jersey, where he has lead development efforts since 2015. Prior to joining Better Tomorrows, Michael supported grant review at the Philadelphia Cultural Fund. In his career, he has also managed foundation and government relations for the Please Touch Museum in Philadelphia and marketing and development consulting for the Athenaeum of Philadelphia. Michael is a graduate of Temple University, where he earned a Master's degree in Art History.

TOGETHER IS BETTER: AFFORDABLE HOUSING THROUGH PARTNERSHIP

Billie Wade
Kentucky Bankers Association HOPE of Kentucky

All banks, regardless of size, should consider becoming involved in lending to or investing in affordable housing projects, particularly those supported by Federal Low-Income Housing Tax Credits ("LIHTC"). Not only does this work provide much needed affordable housing to the community, it provides **CRA** credits for the bank – and it can provide a good earning asset for the bank's balance sheet. For a bank that lacks the expertise in underwriting the credit, partnering with another bank or a banking consortium like **HOPE** of Kentucky can provide that expertise.

LIHTC OVERVIEW

The LIHTC program was implemented through the 1986 Tax Reform Act. It provides for 10 years of Federal tax credits to be allocated to affordable housing projects that comply with IRS regulations of leasing to tenants whose incomes are at or below either 60 percent or 50 percent of Area Median Income.

Unfortunately, there is a perception that these projects are public housing or Section 8 properties, which is not the case. These programs consist of housing where all or a portion of the occupants' housing cost is paid directly by the government. LIHTC properties, on the other hand, do not provide direct payment assistance to the renters, but alternately, the LIHTCs are used to finance the construction, not the operation, of the properties. Unlike public housing, tenants of LIHTC developments tend more to be workforce employees who can make up to $30,000, depending on community average incomes and family sizes. As we often tell bank management, a good portion of your employees will likely qualify to live in a LIHTC property.

The tax credits from LIHTC deals are "sold" to investors, typically larger banks and insurance companies, for prices ranging from $0.80 to over $1.00 per dollar of credit. These investment dollars are injected into the project as equity, typically providing 60 percent to 75 percent of the necessary funding. This allows for permanent loans to be a relatively small part of the financing which enables the rents to be 30 percent or more below comparable market rate projects.

The relatively small amount of leveraging required for LIHTC projects greatly reduces the credit risks in lending to them. In addition, significant reserves are required to be funded by both lenders and investors and available for future needs. A typical project will need at least six months of operating expenses, including debt payments, to be funded into an operating reserve. Also, a repair and replacement reserve of $350 to $400 per unit will be funded annually. This allows for adequate funds to be available for capital needs that typically occur 10 to 15 years after construction is completed.

A 2014 study by a national CPA firm that specializes in LIHTC developments surveyed LIHTC projects since inception of the program in 1986. The cumulative default rate was less than 0.06 percent, much less than any other commercial real estate category. The Office of the Comptroller of the Currency (OCC) referenced that study in 2014 in their publication "Insights," encouraging banks to invest in and/or lend to LIHTC projects. The OCC publication provides a good explanation of how LIHTC works and the legal structure they employ.

THE IMPORTANCE OF A LOAN CONSORTIUM

While many community banks may be interested in participating in LIHTC projects, the application and administration costs of LIHTCs can be burdensome. This is where a loan consortium can become a powerful community development engine.

At HOPE of Kentucky, we have created a consortium of 26 banks from across Kentucky to pool loan funds to make permanent loans on affordable housing projects financed principally utilizing equity generated from the sale of LIHTCs. One of the key benefits for community banks is that they can diversify and limit their overall credit and interest rate risks but still earn the benefits of positive CRA credit and overall community development. A loan consortium like ours allows banks to participate in a highly technical aspect of the affordable housing industry without the need to employ that expertise on their own staff.

WHY IT MATTERS

After the recent Great Recession and beyond, the need for affordable housing has never been greater. A number of studies have identified a large percentage of households paying 50 to 70 percent of their income toward housing related expenses. This leaves little for other needs. In communities throughout the United States, from our largest cities to smaller towns, we are experiencing an affordable housing crisis, which is forcing many people to make difficult choices, including leaving their hometowns for more affordable housing options.

LIHTCs can be a powerful solution to this affordable housing dilemma. LIHTC projects limit household rents and utilities to 30 percent of income. A majority of the properties we work on at HOPE of Kentucky have an average occupancy of 95 percent or higher, many with large waiting lists, further demonstrating the strong demand. The opportunities far outweigh the current capacity.

Given the urgency of our nation's need for affordable housing, LIHTC developments and loan consortiums are an effective way to begin addressing this growing issue on a wide scale. We believe all banks, and thereby their communities, can benefit from lending to or investing in affordable housing projects. It can not only be profitable and provide CRA Credits, but it's one of a few areas where a bank can do well by doing good.

BILLIE WADE is a CPA and former banker who has 20 years of experience in lending and investing in affordable housing projects. He is the Executive Director of HOPE of Kentucky, a nonprofit loan consortium offered through the Kentucky Bankers Association. Prior to joining HOPE of Kentucky, Billie was the President and CEO of Citizens Union Bank. He is active in his community, currently serving in a leadership capacity with the Housing Partnership Inc., and the Collaborative for Teaching and Learning.

WHAT CRA MEANS TO ME:

COMMUNITIES MADE AFFORDABLE

Rob Locke
Habitat for Humanity of Metro Louisville

I know Community Reinvestment Act exams can cause a lot of stress in the life of a banker, but they seriously consider the community investments banks are making. That gives my organization, Habitat for Humanity of Metro Louisville, a seat at the table. Creating affordable housing requires a tremendous amount of capital, and motivated banks make better partners.

Home is a powerful concept. Children of homeowners are 25 percent more likely to graduate from high school, are 116 percent more likely to graduate from college and will earn a 24 percent higher income in their lifetime.[1] Affordable homeownership is very important work because it impacts both the homebuyer and the community. A community with more homeowners creates a more educated workforce, which impacts everyone. Habitat sells all the homes it builds at no profit through no-interest loans so every buyer is invested in affordable homeownership.

The need for affordable housing is significant. In Jefferson County alone, our primary service area, 6,500 public school students are homeless at any given time. About one-third of the Louisville workforce spends more than 30 percent of their income on housing.[2] Just about every family that buys a Habitat home starts out in one of these categories.

Habitat partners with local banks to build a "bankers' house" just about every year. We've been in business for more than 30 years and have built around 25 "bankers' houses." While many folks are involved because they have good hearts and want to support their neighbors, I'm pretty confident every bank's financial contribution and their employees' volunteer hours are provided to their CRA examiner.

As I look through the list of the 25 or so families who've bought "bankers' houses" from Habitat, a few stories come to mind, but I'll limit my narrative to three that have been impacted by this amazing program:

> Zakaria Lado lost part of his hand during the war in Sudan and brought his family to the U.S. more than 15 years ago. His house is one of seven we built in one block of the Smoketown neighborhood. This street feels like a melting

---

[1] Joint Center for Housing Studies of Harvard University, "The State of the Nation's Housing 2013," available at http://www.jchs.harvard.edu/research/publications/state-nations-housing-2013

[2] Metropolitan Housing Coalition, " Living in Community: Housing for People Living with Disabilities and our Aging Population," State of Metropolitan Housing Report, 2016, available at http://metropolitanhousing.org/wp-content/uploads/2016/12/2016-State-of-Metropolitan-Housing-Report.pdf

pot – a few people that grew up in the neighborhood bought there, along with several African immigrants. Zakaria's son Rizzik made the front page of the paper when we were building his house for kicking the winning field goal that sent his high school to the state football championship. Zakaria will pay off his loan in nine years.

Kary Goff bought his "bankers' house" in 2002. Kary is a cook and made a great meal to celebrate his house dedication. At the time we built his home, he was really struggling with his faith and was truly amazed by the volunteers that came out to help him. He credits the Habitat process with "getting him back to church." Soon after he closed on his home, Kary began volunteering as a mentor for troubled youth. He will pay off his loan in five years.

Selena Coomer bought her Habitat home 10 years after Kary in 2012. She is a recovering addict and works as an abuse counselor for The Healing Place, a local nonprofit supporting addiction. Part of her job involves working with a group of recovering women and encouraging them to connect with each other and work through the recovery process. Selena's "class" discovered she was building a Habitat home and became regular construction volunteers, coming out to build her home even when Selena couldn't be on site. Since completing their Habitat home, Selena and her son Jordan have had more success. Selena is now back in school studying to become a nurse and has been promoted at The Healing Place to Director of Health Services. Jordan had the opportunity to travel to Europe to represent Team USA in basketball as a high school sophomore, and is now on track to attend college. Selena will pay off her loan in 15 years.

There are at least 21 more stories like these: times when low-income people of character have used the power of home to improve their lives. And this group only represents the "bankers' houses" homeowners. All in all, our local Habitat will complete its 500th home in 2018. We've also been involved with more than 100 repairs on owner-occupied homes. All of our work is tied to bringing people together to build homes, community and hope. On the state level, nearly 70 percent of Kentuckians own their own home, and about 30 percent rent. In nearly every neighborhood where Habitat families have invested, this ratio is flipped to 30 percent homeownership and 70 percent rental. Every Habitat home helps improve these numbers.

While quality affordable rental housing is a very good thing, many of the landlords in our transitional neighborhoods seem to be more concerned with rent than the value of their property. I've heard of absentee landlords referring to these properties as "disposable houses" and encountered many circumstances where a landlord has no interest in making exterior repairs that would improve the streetscape. (This is not always the case and I am always looking for ways to partner with real estate investors with strategic vision who are willing to invest in neighborhoods.)

Homeowners are often engaged in neighborhood associations or block watches. They have personal "skin in the game" because their largest investment is in their home. Homeowners are more likely to paint their porch posts or plant flowers in their yard. Selena now has chickens in her backyard and shares the eggs with her neighbors. The 2017 "bankers' house" homebuyer invested on her street because her best friend (also a Habitat homeowner) lives next door!

While I'm deeply grateful for each person that chooses to share their time, talent and treasure through the work of Habitat, I am also grateful the Community Reinvestment Act encourages banking institutions to thoughtfully deploy capital in low-income areas of our community. The combination of good intentions and reasonable regulations has helped hundreds of homeowners, dozens of neighborhoods in Louisville and millions throughout the nation.

ROB LOCKE is a native of Louisville, Kentucky and a Centre College graduate who has spent most of his career working for Habitat for Humanity. While he has done most of his work in Louisville, Rob has built Habitat houses in Eastern Kentucky, Guatemala, Tennessee and the Philippines. He ran the construction department of Louisville Habitat for ten years and recently completed his eleventh year in the executive position. Rob is a member of the board of directors of the Housing Partnership, Inc. and has served on the LG&E/KU Community Advisory Panel. He is marred, has two daughters and is a member of Springdale Presbyterian Church.

HOARDING THE AMERICAN DREAM: NIMBYISM AND INHERENT SEGREGATION

Evan Holladay
LDG Development

"It has such a great view! There is a better use for that site. Why put affordable housing THERE?!"

This was heard at a community meeting held for a brand new workforce affordable housing development along the river with views of the city skyline, in a city desperate for reasonably priced housing options. NIMBYism ("Not In My Back Yard") is alive and stronger than ever in communities of all breadths of income, backgrounds and ethnicities, throughout America.

The formation of the Community Reinvestment Act (CRA) and the Low-Income Housing Tax Credit (LIHTC) program have had a significant positive effect in creating and preserving affordable housing for families across America. However, much work still lies ahead to overcome systemic segregation, the "Not In My Backyard" mentality and the severe lack of funding available to create a stronger future for our children and our communities.

Since its inclusion in the Tax Reform Act of 1986, the Low-Income Housing Tax Credit owes much of its success to the Community Reinvestment Act and the requirement that banks invest in all the neighborhoods they serve, including low- to moderate-income communities. States are allocated the tax credits annually from the Federal government, and in turn, competitively award the tax credits to affordable developments. Banks will buy the tax credits with a dollar-for-dollar investment, helping to satisfy their CRA investment requirements and creating or preserving affordable housing.

The Low-Income Housing Tax Credit has helped create or maintain over 2.97 million affordable homes in a time of critical shortage.[1] The public-private partnership (PPP) set up through the tax credit program has also helped to create and sustain around 96,000 jobs annually,[2] with the $8 billion in annual tax credits[3] being leveraged with over $6.6 billion annually in private equity in affordable housing.[4]

---

[1] HUD User, "Low-Income Housing Tax Credits," July 10, 2017, available at https://www.huduser.gov/portal/datasets/lihtc.html#query

[2] Robert Dietz, "How Many People Have Benefitted from the Affordable Housing Credit?" Eye on Housing, November 16, 2015, available at http://eyeonhousing.org/2015/11/how-many-people-have-benefitted-from-the-affordable-housing-credit/

[3] HUD User, "Low-Income Housing Tax Credits," July 10, 2017, available at https://www.huduser.gov/portal/datasets/lihtc.html#query

[4] Daniel Garcia-Diaz, "Low-Income Housing Tax Credit: the Role of Syndicators," U.S. Government Accountability Office, February 16, 2017, available at http://www.gao.gov/assets/690/682890.pdf

So why do we create affordable housing? To give disadvantaged families equal opportunity to live in a safe and quality home in a prosperous neighborhood. The common misconception is that affordable housing is full of individuals who want to take advantage of a "welfare system" and have no desire to excel and live a better life. This is far from true. The people who call affordable housing home are working class members of society. They are your children's pre-school teacher, the server at your favorite restaurant, your nurse or even your local police officer.

In all cities across the United States, there is a constant juggling act for working-class families to cover the bills to afford food, pay their rent or mortgage and, all the while, fight an uphill battle of little to no growth in income. Most working-class families are only one unfortunate event away from disrupting their entire lives (whether it's a broken-down car or two weeks of debilitating sickness) and putting their family at serious risk of losing their housing. Affordable housing and the LIHTC program are working to stop this vicious cycle of generations of poverty and disadvantage.

There is still much needed in the way of progress for equitable housing for all, and despite the continued signs of a strengthening economy, severe housing problems are on the rise and near record highs. In August 2017, the U.S. Department of Housing and Urban Development (HUD) released their Worst Case Housing Needs Report and households classified as having worst case housing needs increased from 7.7 million in 2013 to 8.3 million in 2015, meaning more lower income families are paying more than 50 percent of their income for housing.[5]

---

[5] U.S. Department of Housing and Urban Development and Office of Policy Development and Research, "Worst Case Housing Needs: 2017 Report to Congress," August 2017, available at https://www.huduser.gov/portal/sites/default/files/pdf/Worst-Case-Housing-Needs.pdf

Although the current national housing crisis is getting worse, the problem commenced when our cities first formed their future planning, incorporating exclusionary housing policies, leading to inherent segregation. This has been caused by the over-regulation of our land use policies, designed to protect home values, schools and neighborhoods of the prosperous while fueling a massive distortion in the housing market.[6] This exclusionary zoning is, as Richard Reeves, a Senior Fellow of Economic Studies at the Brookings Institute, puts it, "a form of 'opportunity hoarding' by the upper middle class, a market distortion restricting access to a scarce good (in this case, land), that restricts opportunities (such as good schools) to other children. Those upper middle class voters who oppose more mixed-use housing in their own neighborhoods are what I call 'Dream Hoarders,' keeping elements of the American Dream for themselves at the expense of others."[7]

Continuing this demarcation on where a city can and cannot put workforce housing, local politicians and neighborhood leaders carry an omnipresent vision of NIMBYism. This Not-In-My-Backyard mentality only exacerbates what the exclusionary zoning got started. Because any site that is proposed for use as workforce housing needs some form of community gathering, either for rezoning, funding mandates or to engage the thoughts and ideas of the community, it is likely met with stiff resistance from the public. This often stems from a lack of understanding as to what affordable housing really is, leading it to be seen as the "black eye" of society, resulting in no one wanting affordable housing anywhere near their home. This is where the NIMBY term comes from. And Councilmembers are often held to this view whether they believe it or not because they are under political pressures to

---

[6] Edward Glaeser, "Reforming land use regulations," Brookings Institute Report, April 24, 2017, available at https://www.brookings.edu/research/reforming-land-use-regulations/

[7] Richard V. Reeves, "'Exclusionary Zoning' is opportunity hoarding by upper middle class," Brookings.com, May 24, 2017, available at https://www.brookings.edu/opinions/exclusionary-zoning-is-opportunity-hoarding-by-upper-middle-class/

support what their constituents want, even if it runs counter to what is good for the community as a whole.

With the local and municipal hurdles facing workforce housing, there is also the broad role that Federal funding plays in the creation of workforce housing and the shrinking funding that is allocated to the overarching issue. Over the years, the Federal branch of government responsible for workforce housing and housing equality, HUD, has seen a continual decrease in available funding. Instead of finding an ultimate solution, the current Presidential administration has set forth the goal of cutting the HUD annual budget by 22.16 percent, or $6.82 billion in the next fiscal year. Cutting federal funds would essentially put all funding responsibility for workforce housing creation and neighborhood building on the small shoulders of local municipalities. Given the tight budgetary condition of many cities, most do not prioritize workforce housing, and this opens the door for further NIMBYism from neighborhoods or local political leaders.

With the pivotal role that housing carries in helping to forge the future well-being of families, it is crucial for our country to address the challenges that still lie ahead. Equitable housing must be discussed openly and regularly. It should be considered across all parts of town, including all income levels and ethnicities. Our federal government must invest in workforce housing and local politicians as well as community leaders must make our country's goal for equitable housing for all a priority. Our future generations deserve to live in a quality home with a beautiful view, in the neighborhood of their choice, no matter their income.

EVAN HOLLADAY is the Development Manager for LDG Development where he oversees future multi-family affordable housing deals concentrated on Kentucky and Texas. His responsibilities include site selection, acquisition, feasibility analysis and financing. He is experienced in a variety of development financing including securing Low-Income Housing Tax Credits, obtaining debt financing, managing equity payments and working with asset management. He is a graduate of the University of Louisville with a B.S. in Economics, Entrepreneurship and International Business and also studied at the University of Economics in Prague.

WHAT CRA MEANS TO ME:

A LIFELONG PASSION

Erbi Blanco-True
Gibraltar Private Bank & Trust

I started my banking career in the late 80's as a New Accounts Representative. Despite many years in retail banking, including serving as a Branch Manager for over 10 years at three different institutions, I had never heard of the Community Reinvestment Act. This is hard to believe! I had direct contact with customers; provided and cross-sold services; engaged with different community organizations; and was charged with bringing in new consumer, residential and commercial loans. Yet I was never trained on a key factor affecting the bank's performance relative to all these areas.

So when I started working at the Federal Home Loan Bank of Atlanta ("FHLBA") in 2000 as a Senior Relationship Manager for the state of Florida, I was surprised to hear about CRA, which, amongst other things, encouraged banks to meet the needs of low- and moderate-income ("LMI") residents and geographic areas. I learned that the FHLBA provided several products to help member banks meet their CRA goals and objectives, including the First Time Homebuyer Program, which provides down payment assistance for LMI borrowers; the Affordable Housing Program, which provides subsidies to assist in financing the acquisition, construction, rehabilitation and development of affordable housing; and community investment advances, which offer reduced rate funding that provides critical support for affordable housing and economic development projects. I was excited to learn about all the resources available to help disadvantaged communities.

During a meeting with some of the FHLBA member banks in South Florida, there was discussion of putting together a consortium of banks to finance larger affordable housing projects. Although community banks wanted to participate in these larger deals, specifically Low-Income Housing Tax Credit ("LIHTC") transactions, they didn't feel comfortable with the associated complexities and risk. By partnering with other banks, the risk would be shared and all the participating banks would receive CRA credit. We immediately contacted Neighborhood Lending Partners ("NLP"), an established multi-bank lending consortium located in Tampa, to discuss the possibility of their organization expanding into Southeast Florida. This expansion would eliminate spending the time, energy and money to put together a brand new entity requiring all new infrastructure, policies, procedures, underwriting guidelines, etc.

After months of discussion, attorney's fees and negotiations, Neighborhood Lending Partners of South Florida was created! Since I had been involved in putting together the organization from the beginning, I was selected to become the Executive Director of the new affiliate. Leaving the FHLBA after only two years to join an unknown entity was difficult, but I knew that I had found my life's purpose in this new endeavor. This is when my interest in CRA developed and drove me to ensure NLPSF succeeded so that it would be easier for affordable housing to be created in South Florida.

For those who are not familiar with banking consortia, the member banks make a capital contribution (for which they receive CRA investment credit) which helps to fund the administration of the organization; commit a certain dollar amount to the loan pool (CRA lending credit) which provides the funds to finance the projects; and serve on the organization's board and/or committees (CRA service credit); banks can receive credit for all three CRA performance tests with just one organization. NLPSF was a nonprofit 501(c)3 Community Development Financial Institution ("CDFI"). The loans were made to affordable housing developers from the combined loan pool while NLP's back office in Tampa provided underwriting, servicing, compliance and other administrative functions. It's a bit complicated, but it worked!

This was the most challenging position I had ever held. I was responsible for bringing banks into the consortium to increase our pool, marketing NLPSF to affordable housing developers so we could utilize the pool funds, partnering with community organizations and meeting with government officials who managed local, state and federal housing subsidies, all while managing a budget, a local board made up of the member banks and a relationship with the team at the main office in Tampa. I had to learn all about Low-Income Housing Tax Credits, including how Florida allocated and awarded the Credits, as well as other products and resources that helped fund affordable housing. By attending numerous meetings, conferences and workshops, while reading every document ever created about the subject matter, I eventually became an "expert" in the world of affordable housing finance. I was fortunate to eventually be asked to write articles, speak at events and serve on related boards. Within a short period of time, NLPSF became a great success, attracting over 40 member banks and helping to finance over a thousand units of affordable housing in less than four years. Banks who participated not only received CRA credit, but also received "complex and innovative" consideration for participating in this new collaboration, which provided a creative way to offer affordable housing finance options in South Florida.

The most rewarding part of the whole learning experience was how CRA affected families and neighborhoods. During this time, a housing bubble had created a huge affordable housing crisis in South Florida. The cost of homes was increasing at a rate of up to 20 percent per year in certain areas, while wages remained the same. Miami was rated as one of the cities with the worst "housing cost burden," since the percentage of households paying more than 30 percent of their income for housing costs had exceeded 50 percent of the residents. As many of us in the business know, according to the Department of Housing and Urban Development, households that spend more than 30 percent of their income on rent are "housing-cost burdened." And the heavier that burden gets, the more difficult it is to afford food, utilities and other necessary living expenses.

So it was enlightening to find out that thousands of families in our communities couldn't afford to live here. Having grown up in Miami in the working class neighborhood of Little Havana, from immigrant parents, this idea of "affordable housing" affected me on a personal level. I never knew how much my parents struggled to provide a safe, clean living environment for my brothers and me. I know that they didn't take advantage of any housing programs, but mainly because they were unaware. It was important to me that I help spread information about local housing subsidy programs to everyone who needed them!

This was how CRA became my passion. Serving on several nonprofit boards, and later as Chair of Miami-Dade County's Affordable Housing Advisory Board, I learned so much about the housing needs in our community and how to address them. I met several families who had been awarded apartments at the LIHTC communities we financed who were so grateful to finally have an affordable place to live. Many had been on "waiting lists" for Section 8 and other programs for years. This was a dream come true for them (and me!). While providing financial literacy classes, I met people from all walks of life who had no idea what a mortgage was, how to budget for housing-related expenses or how to save for future needs. It was very rewarding to use my experience in banking, and my knowledge in affordable housing, to help those most in need. All this can be credited to CRA.

Since my years at NLPSF I've led the CRA and Community Development efforts of a community bank for over seven years and now serve as a consultant to help banks meet their CRA requirements. I continue to serve on boards and provide pro bono advice to nonprofit organizations that want to take advantage of CRA regulations to help them meet philanthropic goals. And, I haven't lost the passion for learning, growing and continuing to help the community through the Community Reinvestment Act!

ERBI BLANCO-TRUE is a banking professional with over 30 years of experience in financial services. She currently serves as a CRA Advisor to Gibraltar Private Bank & Trust, specializing in the areas of Community Reinvestment Act compliance, community development, corporate social responsibility and nonprofit outreach. Prior to this, she served as Senior Vice President, Director of CRA & Community Development at Great Florida Bank for over seven years. Erbi also served as Market President of Neighborhood Lending Partners, a multi-bank lending consortium providing financing for affordable housing developments in South Florida. Erbi obtained her Master of Business Administration degree from Florida International University and her Bachelor of Professional Studies degree from Barry University.

LIFE ON THE FINANCIAL EDGE

Chris Blakeley
Credit Fair-e

In America, 47 percent of people are living on the financial edge[1] – just one financial emergency away from being unable to pay their rent, make a car payment or fully feed their family. It's very likely that everyone reading this knows someone in a cash crunch or financial bind. It could be a coworker, a friend, your brother or sister or even you. Millions of these folks, who have no access to emergency funds like savings accounts, credit cards or the ability to borrow from family or friends, are forced to turn to short-term, high-interest loans in a time of financial emergency. These good, hard working people are lured with promises of quick and easy cash and simple, inexpensive repayment terms. In reality, what they get is a spiraling cycle of debt that forces them to re-borrow

---

[1] Federal Reserve Board of Governors, "Report on the Economic Well-Being of U.S. Households in 2015, " May 2016, available at https://www.federalreserve.gov/2015-report-economic-well-being-us-households-201605.pdf

again and again, costing them a total of $21 billion in fees and interest in 2015.

The typical loan for someone in financial distress is a payday loan. These are generally short-term, high-cost loans for $500 or less that borrowers must repay when they receive their next paycheck. Depending on a state's laws, payday loans are usually offered through storefront locations or online. To illustrate a typical payday loan transaction, let's look at the following example:

Brian is a social worker making $32,000 per year. Brian's car breaks down and he doesn't have enough cash on hand to pay the $500 repair bill. Because Brian relies on his car for driving his kids to school and making his daily commute to work, he quickly scrambles to find a source of funds to pay the bill. Unfortunately, Brian has bad credit from some financial trouble a few years back, so he turns to one of the only options he has for money – a payday loan.

Brian borrows the $500 from an online lender who charges $75 in interest for a loan of that size and requires borrowers to repay the full amount using their next paycheck. For Brian, this means he'll have to use 62 percent of his next paycheck to repay the debt. This is devastating to Brian's financial health, as he's forced to take out another payday loan to cover other bills and become trapped in an expensive and harmful debt cycle that costs him additional interest charges and other fees of nearly $600.

Unfortunately, for the millions of Americans using short-term, high-interest credit products, Brian's situation is not an extreme case. The average payday borrower takes out eight loans per year and pays $520 in interest and fees.[2]

---

[2] PEW Charitable Trusts, "Payday Lending in America: Who Borrows, Where They Borrow and Why," July 2012, available at
http://www.pewtrusts.org/~/media/legacy/uploadedfiles/pcs_assets/2012/pewpaydaylendingreportp df.pdf

To be financially *empowered*, a consumer needs access to high-quality financial products and services, sufficient information about choices in the marketplace, the capability to make good financial decisions that benefit themselves and their families and – when required – access to trusted advisors to help navigate a complex financial marketplace. With nearly 100 million low-income and economically vulnerable individuals in the United States[3], financial empowerment is often a foreign concept. Many of these people are either unbanked, underbanked or have thin or no credit files. In addition, these folks tend to be diverse by culture, geography, stage of life and financial status. While initiatives to enhance the financial stability of this population have multiplied and shown promise over the past decade, we have yet to establish a strategy on a national scale that addresses their unique needs for consumer financial products and services.

A study published in November 2013 by the Consumer Financial Protection Bureau[4] takes a close look at empowering low-income and economically vulnerable consumers. It discusses how consumers with low incomes face a number of policy-related, institutional and personal barriers that restrict their access to the financial system. Institutional barriers range from lack of physical access to identification requirements, unaffordable service fees and lack of products that align with their needs. Participants in this study suggested that financial institutions and service providers can pursue several strategies to counteract barriers to accessing basic financial services, including actions to:

---

[3] Consumer Financial Protection Bureau, "Empowering low income and economically vulnerable consumers: Report on a National Convening," November 2013, available at http://files.consumerfinance.gov/f/201311_cfpb_report_empowering-economically-vulnerable-consumers.pdf

[4] Ibid.

- Better understand the needs of the consumer and create products that fit those needs;
- Meet consumers where they are, sometimes away from the branch in the community;
- Engage with partners that already serve low-income consumers to build trust;
- Provide incentives for participation in the mainstream financial system; and
- Craft technology solutions that work for low-income consumers.

Consumers with low incomes are less likely than other consumers to be able to access affordable credit; they often use high-cost alternative products to meet their needs. Several features of the credit market are particularly challenging for many consumers with low incomes. Some of the biggest barriers include their inability to qualify for loans because they have little, poor or no credit history; lack of general understanding about credit and the type of loans that would be most useful; lack of knowledge about how to correct their credit reports or improve their scores; and a general perception that the credit system is inaccessible to them. Participants in the study also reported that consumers could greatly benefit from:

- Increased access to credit reports and scores;
- Specialized financial education; and
- More accessible and affordable products and services that are tailored to fit their credit needs and capacity to repay.

Low- and middle-income Americans are craving better and more affordable financial products. We in the financial services industry owe it to them to design products that meet their specific challenges and help them build stronger financial health. By doing so, we will all contribute to meeting the goals and ambitions of the Community Reinvestment Act.

CHRIS BLAKELY is the Founder and CEO of Credit Fair-e, a company he started in 2014 to provide some of the most vulnerable members of society an opportunity to access fair, affordable financial products. Credit Fair-e strives to be a trusted partner to the emerging middle class by providing affordable small-dollar loans where the loan amount, repayment period, interest rate and fees are structured so the borrower can successfully repay the loan without re-borrowing, while still meeting basic needs and other financial obligations. Prior to creating Credit Fair-e, Chris was the Vice President of Operations and IT at PetFirst Healthcare and has worked for Aegon and Humana. He is a graduate of the University of Louisville with a B.S. in Business Administration and Computer Information Systems and an MBA in Entrepreneurial Studies.

THE FINANCIAL CONTINUUM: ACHIEVING ECONOMIC MOBILITY

Adam Hall
Fifth Third Bank

Throughout my more than 20 year career in banking, I have recognized the importance financial institutions have in helping people live their day-to-day lives. While fewer people are visiting a physical bank branch these days, individuals conduct financial transactions several times a day, whether by using a debit card, making online bill payments or even making person-to-person payments facilitated by apps like Zelle.

As a Community and Economic Development professional, I think one of the most important roles financial institutions can play to assist low- and moderate-income (**LMI**) individuals and families in achieving upward economic mobility is by helping those customers build assets. While income supports play an important role in stabilizing families, programs like TANF and SNAP are not always effective in helping people rise out of poverty.

Asset building, however, can help people move up the economic ladder. As we think about our obligations under the Community Reinvestment Act to make financial services available to low- and moderate-income communities, we need to think beyond the number of branches and ATMs and where they are located.

I like to think about LMI consumers as a part of a financial continuum. Obviously, the first phase of the continuum is to "bank" an unbanked customer, which helps them move away from very costly alternative financial services such as check cashing outfits. This alone is a huge savings for the unbanked, as estimates indicate unbanked people spend up to $40,000 more for financial services over their working life than people who have banking relationships.[1] While moving people away from these services is an important first step, it needs to be viewed as such: The first step in what should be a long-term relationship. The next step is to have conversations with the customer about their goals and some of the ways a bank can help them achieve those goals. I believe, whatever the customer's goals may be, one important role we as bankers can play in helping them achieve their goals is to help them build credit. Whether they want to purchase a home, start a small business, buy a vehicle or even get a better job, credit will factor into any and all of these goals. Having bad credit will make any goal more difficult – and more expensive.

When I talk to a customer about credit-building, I often encounter resistance. Often LMI consumers are reticent to take on debt.

---

[1] U.S. Department of Treasury Office of Financial Education, "Community Financial Access Pilot: Elements of an Effective 'Banking the Unbanked' Strategy," available at https://www.treasury.gov/resource-center/financial-education/Documents/elements_unbanked_strategy.pdf

They either fear they will get in over their head, or they operate under a mentality of "if I cannot afford to pay cash for a purchase, I shouldn't be making it." Those are legitimate concerns for all of us, not just LMI consumers.

In those discussions, I present having excellent credit as a vehicle to maximize your options in any given situation. For example, if your car breaks down and you have a 720 credit score, the auto shop is likely to let you finance repairs, possibly even for 90 days or six months with no interest. Alternatively, if you have a 580 credit score, you will have to pay upfront for the repairs. In that situation, the 720 credit score will give you a range of options from which to make the best financial decision for yourself in that moment. With the 580 score, you have two choices: pay up front or don't get your car fixed. Credit, when approached responsibly, is an asset – and a valuable one.

Often, consumers have no idea where to start in building their credit. Some have had credit in the past, made mistakes and think they will be stuck with poor credit forever. Others have never had credit and are frustrated they are unable to get approved. This is an opportunity to introduce secured lending products to consumers. Secured credit cards are a useful tool in building credit for the first time or rebuilding credit from past mistakes. But it is very important to coach the customer to effectively manage the cards. I strongly encourage people to pay their balances off on a monthly basis to avoid interest charges. The adage that you shouldn't buy what you can't afford still works with credit cards. If you can't pay off your purchases when they are due, opt not to make the purchase. I also emphasize if they are carrying a balance to keep that balance at 30 percent or less of the available credit so they are not damaging their credit score.

Another conversation on the continuum is to leverage matched savings accounts or Individual Development Accounts. The concept of matched savings accounts evolved in the early 1990s to give LMI customers an opportunity to save for a significant asset such as a home, a small business or higher education which would help lift them permanently out of poverty.

Financial institutions play several important roles in helping consumers with IDAs. First, they can provide dollars for the matched portion of the accounts. Typically, for every dollar the consumer saves, they are matched, most typically on a four-to-one basis. Obviously, the match accelerates and in most cases, facilitates the consumer's ability to accomplish their goal, whether that's the purchase of a new home, starting or expanding a small business or pursuing higher education. Additionally, with the match, the individual is building equity in their home or their business, or they don't have to take on additional debt to pursue their education.

The second role a financial institution can play with IDAs is to actually open and house the accounts and provide reporting to the partner organization. This gives banks an opportunity to build a relationship with the account holder, potentially resulting in additional opportunities for other deposit relationships and loans.

Finally, working with the nonprofit IDA sponsor and building a partnership can create new opportunities for service for the bank. These new opportunities could be board service, technical assistance or financial education for their clients. These relationships can improve the bank's CRA performance.

Another exciting new opportunity banks have to help vulnerable customers build assets is to offer the recently approved ABLE (Achieving a Better Life Experience) accounts. ABLE accounts allow for disabled individuals to save for their future needs and not have those funds count as part of their asset test for public benefits. These accounts also allow for family and concerned friends to make deposits to help individuals build their savings. This is an important because so often, disabled people struggle when unexpected events occur because they cannot have more than $2,000 in assets. ABLE accounts can help disabled people build emergency savings and have more security and peace of mind.

Banks play an important role in the lives of our customers, providing access to and security for their money. LMI consumers often may be skeptical of financial institutions, but have the same needs, including access and security, as anyone else. Banks should take extra steps to provide products and services, which can help overcome skepticism and fear LMI consumers may have about developing a banking relationship. Products designed to help them achieve their personal financial goals position banks to be partners in our customer's financial lives. This partnership, I believe, leads to longer and deeper relationships. This creates a win-win-win situation. It is a win for the customer as they achieve their goals. It is a win for the financial institution as it opens up a larger customer base. And it is a win for communities as it provides opportunities to help families achieve prosperity.

ADAM HALL is a community development professional with Fifth Third Bank, where he serves as a Community and Economic Development Manager. He has served on the Mayor's Taskforce on Foreclosure Prevention, the Neighborhood Stabilization Committee, volunteered for Habitat For Humanity, New Directions Housing Corporation's Repair Affair and provided financial education with a wide range of nonprofit and government agencies. He is a member of the Executive Committee for Bank On Louisville and a member of the Board of Directors for Shively Area Ministries, Housing and Homeless Coalition of Kentucky, New Directions Housing Corp, St. Benedicts Center for Early Childhood Education, the Office of Safe and Healthy Neighborhoods Advisory Committee, Louisville Housing Opportunities and Microenterprise Community Development Financial Institution, Smoketown Neighborhood Association and the Governing Committee for the Evansville Promise Zone.

WHAT CRA MEANS TO ME:
HELPING OUR GIRLS FIND THEIR VOICE

Sherry Thompson Giordano
PACE Center for Girls Miami

PACE Center for Girls Miami provides girls and young women, ages 11 to 17, an opportunity for a better future through education, counseling, training and advocacy. The PACE Miami intervention and prevention program assists girls and young women in gaining the skills and knowledge they need to stay out of the state's juvenile justice system, become contributing students to the county's educational system and lead healthy, productive and fulfilling lives. The PACE program is statewide and there are nineteen centers throughout the state of Florida. PACE values all girls and young women, believing each one deserves an opportunity to find her voice, achieve her potential and celebrate a life defined by responsibility, dignity, serenity and grace. The PACE Miami Center is located in a high-risk neighborhood and we work with "at promise" Girls from the poorest neighborhoods in Miami-Dade County. We see the impact of poverty every day with our Girls and their families, including violence, incarceration, physical abuse, drug abuse, sexual exploitation and dropping out of school.

The holistic, strength-based and asset-building PACE program model addresses the needs of girls and has garnered recognition nationally as one of the most effective programs in the country for keeping girls from entering the juvenile justice system and for improving their academic standings. One year after transitioning from PACE, 94 percent of our Girls maintain their higher academic status, 92 percent have no involvement with the juvenile justice system and 88 percent have had no involvement with the juvenile justice system after five years!

As PACE Miami is a new nonprofit in the community, we immediately knew that for us to achieve the outcomes we desire, it was important to partner with financial institutions who have the same drive to better our community and to help break the multi-generational cycle of poverty. PACE Miami wanted true partners – those who not only want to support PACE through funding but also through volunteer support for our program.

The partnerships we have been able to forge because of CRA have been amazing. We have regular financial literacy workshops for our PACE Girls and shortly will offer similar workshops to our Girls' parents and families. Our bank partners are eager to share their stories with our Girls. They discuss job opportunities and future careers that our Girls can easily pursue through commitment, dedication and know-how. Our partners are providing this know-how and our Girls are gaining the confidence to discover their full potential.

Our CRA partners act as "professional mentors" for our Girls. The funding we have received goes to the sustainability of our holistic program focused on educational and behavioral improvement. These partnerships have also given PACE Miami great visibility and presence within our community. This is a priceless gift and an added benefit for our organization and would not have happened in such a timely manner without CRA relationships – all of this has happened in just one year of working with our CRA partners. We intend to expand our partnerships to other financial organizations within Miami-Dade county and grow our CRA outreach – for the betterment of our Girls, their families and our community.

SHERRY THOMPSON GIORDANO is a results-oriented senior executive with demonstrated experience in entrepreneurial, corporate global companies and nonprofit organizations. She has a unique combination of "nonprofit expertise and passion" grounded in 30 years of proven corporate experience in the technology industry. She is honored to have been named a recipient of the National Academy Foundation Advisory Board Champion award in July 2011 and the recipient of the South Florida Digital Alliance's "Universal Access Award" in 2012. In 2013, Sherry joined PACE Center for Girls Miami as the Executive Director. She holds a Bachelor's degree in Business from Stephens College, Columbia, Missouri and attended Oxford University in England and completed coursework in Marketing for Nonprofit Organizations at Radcliffe College, Cambridge, Massachusetts.

FINANCIAL EDUCATION AS IT RELATES TO CRA: SUCCESS OR FAILURE?

Keith Ahronheim
Real Estate Education And Community Housing, Inc.
(R.E.A.C.H.)

As we celebrate the fortieth anniversary of the CRA, I must begin by setting forth one of its primary purposes:

"The Community Reinvestment Act is intended to encourage depository institutions to help meet the credit needs of communities in which they operate, including low- and moderate-income neighborhoods, consistent with safe and sound banking operations." It was enacted by the Congress in 1977 and is implemented by Regulation BB.

The key words above are "...to help meet the credit needs of the communities in which they operate." Implicit in these words is the requirement to lend money to individuals within the communities. But if the individuals in the community have credit profiles that do not fit within "safe and sound banking operations," this primary mission of the CRA fails.

Banks too often express to me the inability to provide loans to individuals and businesses within their assessment area because they were not "sound loans" meeting their underwriting guidelines. My fear is banks can fulfill their CRA obligations and responsibilities by merely indicating, "We tried, but were unable to find bankable borrowers." I do recognize there are banks that are committed to educate and assist individuals and businesses to become stronger borrowers. Often, this assistance has been accomplished by providing grants, either directly or through their foundations, to nonprofit organizations to support financial education and coaching.

Although there are many aspects to CRA, this article is devoted to only one; to wit, has financial education had a positive effect on meeting the credit needs of communities as defined by the CRA? Many lenders have recognized this need and offer financial education and pre-purchase homeownership counseling accessible through the bank's website. In addition, they support HUD-approved nonprofit housing counseling agencies that provide the same services for group classes to fill the gap between the actual costs for counseling and HUD housing grants.

The question I now pose is, "Have these financial education efforts been successful?"

My analysis begins with the U.S. Congress and the Federal Reserve. In 2000, Congress requested the Federal Reserve study the CRA's effectiveness. The report recognized "...the difficulty of determining the CRA's influence on bank behavior..." as one of its conclusions and goes on to say, "Because financial and CRA incentives concurrently exist, it is difficult to separate how much influence should be attributed solely to CRA."[1] Unfortunately, this difficulty continues today.

In 2012, *The Journal of Financial Counseling and Planning*[2] raised the question of whether financial education changes behavior in low-income populations. As stated in their article "Translating Financial Education into Behavior Change for Low-Income Populations," "A number of financial education programs have been developed in recent years to address the financial education needs of low-income populations. However, research measuring the effectiveness of these (financial education) programs has not kept pace." Again, more effective ways to measure the success of financial literacy is needed.

In addition, there was "some" evidence that the amount of financial education received may result in improvement in financial behavior. Such programs had more success with those who began with lower levels of financial behavior. Given this finding, the real question becomes, "Even if this group improved, did the improvement rise to the level required to obtain credit?" (An interesting sidebar was that many of the training staff was low paid and having difficulty with their own personal finances.) That leads one to ask, "Who are the most effective counselors?" Are the best counselors ones who are most like the attendees or ones who the attendees can look up to as financially successful role models or ones with formal training? My experience as an attorney

---

[1] Darryl E. Getter, "The Effectiveness of the Community Reinvestment Act, " Congressional Research Service, January 7, 2015, available at
https://www.newyorkfed.org/medialibrary/media/outreach-and-education/cra/reports/CRS-The-Effectiveness-of-the-Community-Reinvestment-Act.pdf

[2] Angela C. Lyons, Yunhee Change and Erik Scherpf, "Translating Financial Education into Behavior Change for Low-Income Populations," Journal of Financial Coaching and Planning, Vol. 17, November 2, 2006, available at
https://papers.ssrn.com/sol3/papers.cfm?abstract_id=2232122

leads me to believe attendees learn best from those who are financially successful and properly trained.

In January 2015, the Congressional Research Service submitted a new report on the effectiveness of the CRA to Congress.[3] This report includes a section on the Congressional debate as to whether the CRA and subsequent amendments create incentives for banks to lend to unqualified borrowers, which may lead to losses. It also postulates that CRA is not providing enough incentives to increase the availability of credit, thus impeding economic recovery following the recession of 2007-2009. It further reasons there are other factors that influence banks' actions, policies and procedures when determining lending decisions to low- to moderate-income households.

In today's world, there is a movement towards financial coaching. I believe this approach is more meaningful, which will provide better results allowing success and effectiveness to be more easily tracked. Results of financial coaching are assessed through changes in three factors: credit score, amount of outstanding debt and amount of savings.

The Consumer Financial Protection Bureau (CFPB)[4] published findings in October 2016 that found coaching can help increase financial well-being. The CFPB based their findings on a research brief entitled *Financial Coaching: A Strategy to Improve Financial Well-Being*[5] and a practitioner brief entitled *Implementing Financial Coaching: Implications for Practitioners.*[6]

---

[3] Darryl E. Getter, "The Effectiveness of the Community Reinvestment Act, " Congressional Research Service, January 7, 2015, available at
https://www.newyorkfed.org/medialibrary/media/outreach-and-education/cra/reports/CRS-The-Effectiveness-of-the-Community-Reinvestment-Act.pdf

[4] Consumer Financial Protection Bureau, "Financial Coaching: A Strategy to Improve Financial Well-Being," October 20, 2016, available at https://www.consumerfinance.gov/data-research/research-reports/financial-coaching-strategy-improve-financial-well-being/

[5] Ibid.

As it relates to the primary directive of the CRA, the CFPB findings indicate:

1. Access to financial coaching resulted in measurable gains for the low- and moderate-income consumers in three areas:
    a. Money management
    b. Objective financial health metrics (savings, debt and credit score)
    c. Subjective feelings of financial confidence
2. Consumers have different levels of engagement in coaching based on needs
3. Financial coaching is customized to meet each person's goals

The CFPB in June 2017 issued another research report, *CFPB Data Point: Becoming Credit Visible.*[7] One of their conclusions is, "...consumers in lower-income areas are much more likely [than those in higher-income areas] to have their credit record created as the result of a third-party debt collection account or some other non-loan item, including a public record." Restated, lower-income consumers are more likely to become credit visible due to negative records such as a debt in collection.

As this finding relates to financial coaching, it demonstrates the initial baseline for low- to moderate-income individuals is different than other income classifications. As such, any financial coaching must be adjusted accordingly. It is important to include coaching

---

[6] Consumer Financial Protection Bureau, "Implementing financial coaching: Implications for practitioners," Practitioner Brief, October 2016, available at https://s3.amazonaws.com/files.consumerfinance.gov/f/documents/102016_cfpb_Implementing_Financial_Coaching_Implications_for_Practitioners.pdf

[7] CFPB Office of Research, "CFPB: Data Point: Becoming Credit Visible," Consumer Financial Protection Bureau, June 2017, available at https://s3.amazonaws.com/files.consumerfinance.gov/f/documents/BecomingCreditVisible_Data_Point_Final.pdf

on rebuilding credit, rather than building a credit profile or increasing a good credit score. This process normally increases the time to reach the level of "safe and sound banking operations" that will enable the individual to access bank credit.

Finally, the CFPB has researched the factors that make financial education effective and increase a consumer's financial well-being.[8] They are:

1. Know the individuals and families to be served;
2. Provide actionable, relevant and timely information;
3. Improve key financial skills;
4. Build on motivation; and
5. Make it easy to make good decisions and to follow through on them.

So where does this leave us with respect to the CRA's mission and purpose? Financial education in and of itself is most effective when it is coupled with additional follow-up. This is where financial coaching comes in. In 2016, the *Financial Coaching Consensus Report* indicated financial coaching has a very quick and dramatic positive effect, which is easily measured through credit score, savings and debt.[9] This report indicates, "The vast majority of funders (77 percent), managers (69 percent) and coaches (78 percent) report that financial coaching improves their clients' financial situations."

Not to over simplify, but effective financial empowerment through financial education and coaching enables individuals to properly budget and determine if they have a deficit or savings at the end of each month. Financial coaches can easily work with people to set

---

[8] Consumer Financial Protection Bureau, "Effective financial education: Five principles and how to use them," June 2017, available at
https://s3.amazonaws.com/files.consumerfinance.gov/f/documents/201706_cfpb_five-principles-financial-well-being.pdf

[9] Asset Funders Network, "Financial Coaching Census 2016: A Progressing Field of Practice," 2016, available at http://assetfunders.org/documents/AFN-Financial_Census2016.pdf

reachable financial goals to adjust their expenses and/or take steps to increase their income. Once an individual has additional disposable income, they can reduce their outstanding debt. This reduction in debt, with proper credit building counseling, will increase their credit scores. Higher credit scores will result in more available credit at lower interest rates with more credit options for the consumer. Simultaneously, the individual will have the ability to increase savings. Finally, as an advocate for homeownership, increasing one's credit score, decreasing non-mortgage debt and increasing savings will result in a profile considered to be a "safe and sound banking" profile – thus a win/win for consumers, depository institutions, lenders and communities.

It is clear to me that one of the most effective ways for depository institutions to obtain positive consideration on their CRA examinations is to support financial education coupled with financial coaching. This empowerment of individuals will result in banks ultimately being able to meet the lending and credit needs of their assessment areas. The current void experienced in many communities can easily be filled by partnering with nonprofit organizations to provide effective financial empowerment.

Banks should be positive and proactive to work towards ensuring their communities' credit needs are met by working to ensure that individuals and businesses in their target areas become safe and sound borrowers.

It is my conclusion that financial education coupled with financial coaching is an effective tool and a necessary requirement in today's environment to "meet the credit needs of the community" as required by CRA.

KEITH AHRONHEIM is the full-time in-house General Counsel for R.E.A.C.H. a 501(c)(3) nonprofit HUD-approved housing counseling agency. He is a member of the NYS Bar, former New York State (NYS) Bar, NYS Administrative Law Judge and professional banker with over 30 years of experience. Before coming to R.E.A.C.H., Keith was a Vice President with JPMorgan Chase Bank managing their Homeownership Center. He is currently the Treasurer of his PGA Homeowner Association; serves on the Executive Committee of the Homeless and Housing Alliance of Palm Beach Count; serves on the Public Policy committee of the Palm Beach County Housing Leadership Council; serves on the executive leadership council of Palm Beach State College; and is a volunteer captain at The Honda Classic.

CREDIT WHERE CREDIT IS DUE

Lori Pollack
Financial Counseling Association of America

At its core, the Community Reinvestment Act is intended to ensure that financial institutions meet the unique needs of the communities they serve. The CRA is about more than just making loans; it's also about educating consumers and helping bring a sense of financial awareness to their lives. This awareness not only helps their families, but also extends to the communities where they live.

For financial institutions, this could mean they provide services such as housing counseling or other forms of financial education directly to the public. Or it could mean that they partner with local subject matter experts to deliver these services directly to consumers.

In many cases, the local subject matter experts are credit counseling agencies, typically nonprofit organizations that work on the front lines combatting financial illiteracy. These agencies attempt to remedy the damage done to its victims, whose lack of financial knowledge often betrays them in critical situations. Among the menu of services provided by credit counseling agencies are federally mandated bankruptcy counseling and debtor education programs, foreclosure counseling, reverse mortgage counseling and free community education. These services not only help individual consumers, they also help the community where each newly educated consumer resides. And of course, these programs often ultimately benefit financial institutions and their CRA programs, since many consumers who regain their financial stability will return later as customers for savings accounts, loans, mortgages and other bank products. Win, win, win.

Many are not familiar enough with credit counseling to be able to distinguish it from other sectors of the debt relief space. The Financial Counseling Association of America (FCAA) is a 501(c)(3) nonprofit trade association whose members are credit counseling agencies, the overwhelming majority of which are also 501(c)(3) nonprofits, which means they share a mission of providing financial counseling and education to the public. FCAA member agencies take a holistic approach in addressing an individual's financial situation, fully reviewing the consumer's financial circumstances before presenting any appropriate options that might be used to resolve the situation. Our counselors review credit reports and create workable Action Plans that help consumers realize the fundamental differences between "needs" and "wants," re-orienting their spending priorities in a way that allows the consumer to pay down their debt, safely and responsibly.

Our members provide a variety of services to help the financially distressed consumer get back on the road to financial well-being, including:

- *Consumer credit counseling:* From budgeting to credit reports to dealing with accounts in collections, FCAA member agencies will develop an Action Plan specific to the consumer based on his or her income, expenses and goals;

- *Debt Management Plans (DMPs):* Unlike debt settlement, which can severely damage a person's credit, DMPs typically allow qualified consumers to repay their principal balances in full, but at significantly lower interest rates. This can give consumers the necessary breathing room in their budgets to help get them back on track;

- *Housing counseling services:* From free foreclosure-prevention and loan-modification services to mandated reverse mortgage counseling, first-time homebuyer classes and rental education, our HUD-certified agencies work with consumers to educate them on buying, maintaining and protecting their homes;

- *Bankruptcy counseling:* Many FCAA agencies are also approved by the Executive Office for United States Trustees to provide pre-filing counseling sessions and pre-discharge debtor education, both of which are required in the bankruptcy process;

- *Student loan counseling:* Certified counselors at FCAA member agencies provide holistic counseling to individuals dealing with student loan debt. Counselors will review all of the expenses impacting the consumer's budget and help them identify and understand the various federal loan repayment options they're eligible for; and

- *Financial education services:* FCAA agencies provide free financial literacy classes throughout their local communities. Many offer programs specifically designed for students, veterans, senior citizens, first-time homebuyers and inmates returning to society, and employee assistance programs.

The services our members offer are desperately needed in communities around the country. While some of these services are provided for a fee, those fees are highly regulated by the states and help cover the cost of the work the credit counseling agency does to fulfill its mission.

So where does agency funding come from? There are occasional grants from individual banks, but there is no government funding for credit counseling services. Many agencies also receive some level of grant money directly from the creditors they work closely with, but those donations have been in steady decline for more than a decade. A great source of support comes from the Community Reinvestment Act, through funds targeted for particular communities and specific programs.

One FCAA member used CRA investment to start a statewide Individual Development Account (IDA) Network. IDAs are matched-savings programs that allow low-income families to save a specified amount of money to be used for buying a home, funding post-secondary education or starting a small business, with the state matching the amount saved by the consumer. Finding synergy between savings and financial education, the counseling agency was able to expand the CRA-supported services to include financial education.

The early results? Over 1,200 households participated in the IDA program. Of the program's participants, 232 people have saved enough to buy their first home; 220 households have made withdrawals to fund a small business; and 1,128 households have made education-related withdrawals. That's a lot of good for a lot of families.

For many credit counseling agencies, CRA has been a true lifeline. Many agencies use their CRA donations and grants to provide free one-on-one counseling and financial education to the community. One particular FCAA member agency uses CRA investments to help underwrite the free financial literacy classes they provide every year to thousands of inmates preparing to re-enter society and to veterans who are successfully overcoming homelessness. The result? Recidivism rates have dropped, and veterans have been able to return to independent living, confident in their financial abilities for the first time.

This is just a small window into the use of CRA support by credit counselors. Many of us watch daily as rumors swirl regarding the fate of CRA – will it apply to fintech charters (if, in fact, charters are given to fintech companies)? Will tax reform kill CRA entirely? The Community Reinvestment Act is vital to helping individuals achieve their goals and critical to the many credit counseling agencies that work so diligently to help strengthen the foundation of the communities they serve. It would be a shame to see this lifeline that has served so many, so well, disappear.

Happy 40th Anniversary, CRA... and many more!

LORI POLLACK is the Executive Director of the Financial Counseling Association of America (FCAA). Established in 1994, the FCAA is a national trade association. Its members are credit counseling agencies, providing consumer credit counseling, housing counseling, student loan counseling, bankruptcy counseling, debt management plans and various financial education services to consumers. FCAA member agencies work diligently to help financially distressed consumers bank on the road to financial well-being.

OUTSTANDING: HOW WE BRING EDUCATION AND HOMEOWNERSHIP HOME

Garry Throckmorton
eHome America

It was 1979 and the **VP** of consumer lending was making the rounds telling us there was a new regulation called the Community Reinvestment Act, and examiners would be visiting soon and possibly asking us some CRA-related questions. I don't remember how he coached us, but through an interesting turn of career-related events, by the mid-1980s I was a consultant coaching bankers on CRA compliance. It was the period when examiners evaluated banks' *processes* for helping meet the credit needs of low- and moderate-income (**LMI**) neighborhoods, rather than what it is today: an evaluation of a bank's actual **CRA** *results* and *impact* compared to peers.

Back then, banks were on their own to develop special loan products and programs aimed at LMI borrowers and neighborhoods, and by the mid-1990s, when I was managing CRA for a large bank, CRA success was not only about results; examiners also looked for innovation in CRA programs and products. By then, the bank where I had managed CRA had become a *large* bank, and fortunately, I discovered that both opportunity and innovation could come from partnering with strong nonprofit organizations – the ones assisting LMI persons and families that desired to work with the bank. This turned out to be a key factor in the bank receiving an "Outstanding" CRA rating.

One of these organizations was Community Ventures (CV), a nonprofit Community Development Financial Institution (CDFI) and NeighborWorks America network member based in Lexington, Kentucky. The agency made such an impression on me that after 30 years in banking, when I had the opportunity to join CV, I jumped at the chance. While I knew the organization from a banker's view, as I experienced firsthand the challenges that a nonprofit CDFI faces in serving a statewide urban and rural customer base, the amount of creativity and innovation required to be successful was truly eye-opening.

And true to the saying, "necessity is the mother of invention," CV was challenged with creating a solution for providing homebuyer and homeowner education services to customers who are unable to attend in-person classes. The goal: making homeownership education available online, 24/7, so customers could access important and beneficial information at times convenient to them and at their own pace, coupled with an hour-long follow-up telephone session with a HUD-certified advisor. eHome America was the answer.

eHOME AMERICA HISTORY AND BENEFITS

While eHome America was originally intended for CV customers only, it wasn't long before other NeighborWorks America member organizations heard about the program and requested to use it to address the same challenge they were facing. And so the eHome Network of partner organizations was born. Within one year of its development in 2009, eHome America was launched as a national program. Today, the course is endorsed by NeighborWorks America and USDA Rural Development and meets the education requirements for special mortgage and down payment assistance programs offered by major lenders across the nation, including state and local Housing Finance Agencies, Freddie Mac, Fannie Mae, the Federal Housing Agency, the Federal Home Loan Bank and many others.

As a CRA-qualified service, eHome is a "game-changer" for assisting bank customers. Banks partnering with eHome Network organizations now have an online option for providing industry standard homeownership education. Previously, these organizations could offer education for customers only through in-person classes.

In the eight years since its inception, eHome America has assisted over 300,000 customers through its network of over 500 partner organizations including many bank partners, operating in all 50 states and three U.S. Territories. It also stands as the education option of choice for Millennial homebuyers who prefer online engagement to in-person classes and frequently access other services through online resources.

Building on its foundation of homeownership education, eHome America has expanded its offerings with additional online courses covering such topics as personal financial management (eHome Money), how first-time homebuyers (now in their new homes) can succeed as homeowners (eHome Post Purchase) and important information about the foreclosure process and options for saving your home when experiencing financial hardship (eHome Foreclosure). Together these courses make up the eHome America online education platform – a valuable community impact resource for banks and their customers.

Interestingly, and in keeping with the phrase, "knowledge is power," banks whose customers take the eHome America homebuyer education course and connect with an advisor afterwards experience, on average, less serious delinquency and default compared to similar mortgage borrowers who don't get homeownership education or advising, and several independent studies support this assertion, including: [1]

- First-time homebuyers who receive education and counseling had a 29 percent reduction in a delinquency rates;
- Borrowers who received education and counseling had significant increases in their credit scores and/or had improved overall credit health;
- Borrowers are better able to measure their "ability to pay" and select better loan products; and
- Counseled borrowers are 67 percent more likely to remain current on their mortgages.

Whether it's a loan retained in the bank's portfolio or sold to an investor (with or without recourse), the whole industry benefits from financially educated borrowers. Stated differently, homeownership education and counseling is a key factor in avoiding future financial crises like the one we've just experienced.

---

[1] Doug Dylla and Dean Caldwell-Tautges, "Moving First-Time Buyers Off the Fence: Solving the Millennial Homebuyer Puzzle with Proven Online Solutions and Partnerships," Federal Reserve Bank of St. Louis, Bridges, Summer 2016, available at
https://www.stlouisfed.org/publications/bridges/summer-2016/moving-first-time-buyers-off-the-fence

In terms of meeting CRA requirements, eHome is a perfect fit. 91 percent of eHome America customers are first-time homebuyers. 61 percent have incomes below $75,000 (well within low- and moderate-income ranges for most areas). 60 percent are under 35 years old, and 35 percent are minority. With CRA's target population clearly being reached, partnering with eHome America is a "win-win" opportunity for banks. Supporting, promoting or encouraging bank customers to get quality homeownership education is sure to receive positive consideration during CRA evaluations.

eHOME AMERICA DESIGN AND IMPACT

So, why is the program effective?

For starters, eHome's homebuyer education course not only meets HUD's homebuyer education core curriculum requirements, but also exceeds the National Industry Standards for Homebuyer Education and Counseling (homeownershipstandards.org). To be sure, the education provided by eHome is of the highest quality available.

Second, the course presents the information in an engaging and easy to understand format, using multiple adult learning techniques. It covers the key aspects of home buying and loan underwriting requirements, leading to better-informed borrowers and smoother loan processing and closing. The course can be accessed by a PC and is fully compatible with smartphones and tablets. Customers can log in and out as often as they like, and the information continues to be available to them even after they close on their home loans.

Finally, the eHome America business model has two primary "pillars." The first pillar is connecting customers to a local agency that provides homeownership counseling or advising. Each eHome

Network agency partner has a unique Internet URL (i.e., "portal") where customers can register and maintain access to a local resource, both now and in the future, should they experience financial hardship at a later time. Delivering this level of personalized service, the program is much more than just some website providing information.

Currently, over 500 organizations and their lender partners nationwide provide eHome America homeownership education and advisory services to customers. These HUD-certified agencies sign up for the program and then incorporate the use of online education into their service-delivery models and promote its use to lender partners. This quality online homeownership education, followed by one-on-one follow-up advising (typically by telephone), is acceptable to HUD and greatly expands the number of customers that can be served efficiently.

While some bankers believe this HUD model will slow down the mortgage loan process, these concerns have proven to be unfounded. In practice, when loan officers and originators alert borrowers to the requirement in a timely manner, it hasn't slowed the process at all. For example, eHome America's largest lending partner, California Housing Finance Agency (CalHFA), processes between 500 and 600 loans a month, all of which require both online education and the one-on-one follow-up session. Since launching eHome, no issues have been reported from either lenders or their customers in getting CalHFA mortgage loan products. In fact, customer feedback has been overwhelmingly positive.

The second pillar of eHome America's business model is a very generous revenue share feature. Developed by a nonprofit organization that understands the financial challenges associated with "nonprofit sustainability," eHome's program is designed to help support eHome's Network partner agencies' operations. The eHome America homebuyer education course (English and Spanish) is priced at $99. eHome America retains $25 for administrative costs, while $74 is returned to the network agency at the end of each month to help offset the costs associated with the one-on-one follow-up advisory session. There's a similar revenue share with the other courses, as well, and the impact of this revenue share feature is significant. For example, as of June 2017, eHome Network partner support totaled $2.5 million for the year, and over $12.5 million has been disbursed since 2010.

While banks provide financial support to homeownership advisory agencies, eHome America's revenue-share feature supports a solid case for banks to receive CRA-qualified investment credit for financially supporting eHome America directly. By promoting eHome America education to mortgage loan customers through specific agency partners, it increases course volume and the associated revenue. At least two eHome Network agency partners each receive more than $100,000 annually in unrestricted dollars from eHome America. This is due in large part to lending partner support of the program, and obviously constitutes a major source of revenue in support of these organizations.

As real estate agents and lenders have continued to increase their understanding of the benefits that accrue to prospective homebuyers that receive quality homeownership education and advisory services, a significant number of individuals and families are now being impacted. While this is both exciting and encouraging, HUD says that out of the estimated 2 million first-time homebuyers annually, less than 10 percent of them are receiving any type of pre-purchase education or advising. There's much work still to be done.

GARRY THROCKMORTON is eHome America's Vice President of Business Development, a division of Community Ventures, a nonprofit Community Development Financial Institution and NeighborWorks American charter member based in Lexington, Kentucky. Prior to joining Community Ventures, Garry worked in banking for 30 years and held positions with Bank One, The Federal Home Loan Bank of Cincinnati, Republic Bank & Trust Company and J.S. Barefoot & Associates, a bank consulting firm. As a bank practitioner, he has extensive experience in regulatory compliance and CRA management. Garry joined Community Ventures in 2008 and has directed the company's lending programs, including the SBA 504 Programs, and served as eHome America's national administrator and as the company's bank relationship manager for both the American Dream Loan Fund and the Bank Enterprise Award programs.

INCUBATE OR ACCELERATE: CREATING JOBS BY CREATING BUSINESSES

Tony Schy
Vistage International

Never heard of an incubator, accelerator or entrepreneur center? You're not alone. They have popped up in towns small and large across the entire country. But you can easily miss them if you are not a budding entrepreneur or business owner.

They have a variety of objectives, but typically support entrepreneurs in their quest to build the next great company. Some of these entities are for-profit. Of those, some have well-aligned incentives with the success of the entrepreneurs they serve, while others are simply selling a support product or tool to that community. Other entities are not-for-profit, and typically have a primary goal of "doing good" by helping to create opportunities for individuals to make it on their own.

Not all young companies fit the mold that you see sensationalized in movies or other pop culture outlets. In fact, most of them are not these idealized stereotypes; they're just regular businesses started by normal people to do something that the market needs. They are not in a wildly unknown field, or creating a new market. This means that they have a wide variety of needs and as a result, need a wide variety of programs to support the various types of companies that are in their infancy.

The majority of young companies start a business with a reasonably well-understood business model. There are other businesses around (whether locally, regionally or nationally) that are substantially similar. These types of businesses include HVAC/plumbing/electrical companies, restaurants, retailers, medical/dental practices, traditional marketing companies, software development firms and a wide range of franchise businesses, just to name a few. Ultimately, they are not reinventing the wheel, but are drafting off of others that have gone before them and figured out how a particular business model works. They may have a minor tweak to the process or price, or deliver their product or service differently, or provide a higher level of customer service than is typical, but the core business model is known.

On the other hand, you have the more traditional idea of a startup. The term "startup" typically refers to new companies that are in a "new business model" category where the product or service is meeting a new need, or solving a problem in a substantially new way. The common element is that the underlying business model – knowing if you will have enough customers willing to pay for what you provide so you can make a reasonable profit – is not well understood.

In this situation, the business owner has to do everything that the owner of a more understood business model has to do in order to get started. But, prior to most of that, they also have to determine if they have a viable business model or not. If they do not, they need to adjust (also know as "pivoting") one or more components of their business model until they have converted their understanding from unknown to known. The additional work required to launch a business with an <u>unknown</u> business model requires more support. This expanded need is where programs such as incubators and accelerators can thrive.

Incubator and accelerator programs can guide the company founder through a process to validate their business model before investing significant time and capital in a business that's likely to fail. The process also serves as a test for someone that would like to start a business. The fantasy of starting your own business so that you can "call the shots" and set your own schedule are often replaced with harsh realities, leading some to reconsider their decision to start a business at all.

The term "accelerator" has come to represent a wide variety of programs that support "early stage" entrepreneurs. These programs focus on entrepreneurs that are just taking the first steps. In some cases, they have jumped in full-time, but many are doing it as a "side hustle" while holding down a day job. The goal of an accelerator program is to provide education and focus on breaking through the first significant milestone – initial validation of a business model. It should help the entrepreneur focus on the things that matter the most and not get distracted by things that are easy or that they are comfortable doing that may prevent the business from moving forward.

For more mature startups, accelerator programs focused on entrepreneurs that have gotten over the first (of several) key milestones are available. These companies are referred to as "early scaling." They likely have the basics of a business model proven, albeit with only modest hard proof. They need another layer of education and re-focusing on a new short list of the things that matter to scale the business. They may also need the support of specialized mentors and connectors who can make introductions to customers, channel partners and investors that could be instrumental in the future of the business.

Incubators are programs or facilities that are usually less programmatic and more facility-based. They provide infrastructure and support services while the entrepreneur is executing their business model. Entrepreneurs in incubators can be at virtually any stage of development, and the services are usually provided for a below-market fee.

When an entrepreneur starts a company, it could be for any number of reasons. But for a community, the reason to support entrepreneurs is clear: job creation.

All of these programs directly and indirectly support local job creation, most often in the form of small businesses. A key statistic that is hard to overlook is that young companies create nearly all net-new jobs.[1] To restate that from a different perspective, if we rely upon mature companies, there will be virtually no job growth, only jobs shifting between companies as some grow, some shrink or die and others introduce automation.

So, while it is important for communities to support mature companies in maintaining the base of jobs for their citizens, they must also embrace the creation and nurturing of young companies

---

[1] Jason Wiens and Chris Jackson, " The Importance of Young Firms for Economic Growth," Ewing Marion Kauffman Foundation, September 13, 2015, available at http://www.kauffman.org/what-we-do/resources/entrepreneurship-policy-digest/the-importance-of-young-firms-for-economic-growth

if they seek overall expansion of the jobs market over the long term.

At the end of the day, the whole startup ecosystem is designed to help entrepreneurs start something new... whatever it might be. And the most successful ecosystems have a variety of programs that allow the entrepreneur to be at any stage in their journey, at any level of experience, with a range of available resources. Ultimately, the ecosystem needs to be there when, where and how the entrepreneur needs support, because the long-term success of a growing economy is dependent on young companies to create jobs as America's newest small businesses.

TONY SCHY is a Vistage Chair and leads CEOs and senior business leaders in monthly confidential peer advisory board meetings to get unbiased input about the challenges they face and to maximize potential opportunities. He also provides private executive coaching tailored to meet individual needs. Prior to his current role, Tony was the Co-Founder and COO of SimCave, a digital gaming arena offering custom video game experiences in an immersive social setting. He is an active Angel Investor investing in both start-up companies and real estate. Tony graduated with a B.S. in Mechanical Engineering from the Rose-Hulman Institute of Technology and currently lives in Sellersburg, Indiana with his lovely wife and two wonderful kids.

WHAT CRA MEANS TO ME:

INDEPENDENCE THROUGH JOB SKILLS

Evelyn McPherson
Blue River Services

BR Grafix, a division of Blue River Services, Inc. (BRS), is truly grateful to be a recipient of community support from local banks. BRS was founded in 1959 by six families who believed that all people are capable of learning when given the opportunity and appropriate support services. With this guiding philosophy and the support from local community partners, BRS is fulfilling its mission to further the independence of people with disabilities and the general public through support programs and resources for all income levels and ages, from infants to seniors, in all areas of life and at all levels of ability.

As a private, 501(c)(3) nonprofit organization, the official mission of Blue River Services is to assist people with disabilities in realizing maximum personal growth and development in home, work and community by providing a continuum of individualized services and supports in settings least restrictive for the needs of the individual. As an adjunct to these services, whenever possible, Blue River Services, Inc. will serve the similar needs of the general community by providing services in non-segregated, community-based settings which emphasize the integrated inclusion of people with disabilities into all areas of life which are enjoyed by members of the community.

In 1990, the agency developed a screen-printing program to provide a training facility and work opportunities for adults with disabilities. Today, this program has grown into a full-fledged commercial screen print shop and storefront known as BR Grafix, located in historic downtown Corydon, Indiana. The shop produces customized apparel and offers embroidery services for communities throughout Southern Indiana.

In a recent effort to improve the production process at BR Grafix, we were seeking funds to purchase a Laser Alignment Wizard® to use in conjunction with our heat press equipment. The laser alignment equipment ensures the consistent and accurate positioning of heat pressed numbers, names, etc. onto shirts and other apparel. Many of the orders that we do for local schools include cutting vinyl to heat press athletes' names on the back of their jerseys and uniforms, and the manual process we had been using was inefficient and sometimes led to costly mistakes.

Using a new fundraising website, we posted online about our need for the laser alignment machine, and were also able to share this online listing with a few local bankers. After just a couple of weeks, the production crew at BR Grafix was overjoyed to hear that First Harrison Bank (FHB) in Corydon, Indiana was interested in supporting us. Their funding made it possible to purchase the laser alignment equipment, which greatly improved the efficiency of our heat pressing and also gave our staff the chance to learn and be trained on a new machine.

On behalf of **BRS** we want to thank **FHB** for their continued support of our agency and the people that we serve.

We're also very thankful for the online fundraising tool that helped us share our story efficiently and connect with the support we needed. As a former banker, I have a deep appreciation for the time and energy it takes to find community projects that meet the financial institution's obligations required by the Community Reinvestment Act. The website that helped us connect with a local banker is truly awesome!

It's a pleasure to share the success of this coordinated effort, where so many different parties came together to meet a need in our community. We are extremely thankful to all those who contributed. The community support we received helps our agency to fulfill our motto: "People Serving People."

EVELYN MCPHERSON is Director of BR Grafix, a Division of Blue River Services, Inc. Prior to working for BRS she worked for 21 years at The Farmers State Bank in Lanesville, Indiana serving as the Data Processing Officer. She is a member of the Lanesville United Methodist Church, where she serves as the Chair of the Administrative Council and Financial Secretary, President of the Corydon Lions Club, member of the Corydon Rotary Club and Trustee of the Lanesville Protestant Cemetery.

STORYTELLING MATTERS: SHARING YOUR CRA EFFORTS DURING EXAMS

Kristen Stogniew, Sarah Oliver & Perin Bush
Saltmarsh, Cleaveland & Gund CPAs and Consultants

In our business of providing Community Reinvestment Act self-assessments and related consultation to our community bank clients, we see the common daily challenges they face. In its 2010 Community Banking Study, the FDIC described community banks as those who provide and depend upon long-term relationship banking; banks whose majority of core deposits are local; and those with a "specialized knowledge of their local community."[1] Community banks tend to make many of their loans to local businesses, and they generally serve cookies in their lobbies.

---

[1] Federal Deposit Insurance Corporation, "FDIC Community Banking Study," December 2012, available at https://www.fdic.gov/regulations/resources/cbi/report/cbi-full.pdf

(Okay, the cookies were not mentioned in the study, that's just a well-accepted fact.)

Under the CRA, a community bank will typically be identified as a small or intermediate-small bank, which means that in the prior two calendar years, their asset size was below $307 million or $1.226 billion, respectively.[2] Depending on previous ratings and other factors, community banks are examined by prudential banking regulators every three to five years. During a CRA examination, regulators determine how well they believe the bank is meeting the needs of the community in which it serves. Seems simple enough, right?

In actuality, it isn't simple at all. In 2016, prudential regulators completed 79 CRA examinations of banks below one billion dollars in asset size.[3] Only eight of these institutions received the coveted *Outstanding* rating, while 70 received a rating of *Satisfactory*. For those doing the math, one institution was told it *Needs to Improve.*

Most of our clients are happy to receive a Satisfactory rating, which in itself is no small task. CRA is not a noun, but rather an action. In the time between examinations, community banks are hitting the pavement and having constant conversations and discussions within their walls and out in the community on ways they can ensure that they are meeting the credit needs of low- and moderate-low income (LMI) individuals and areas. In addition to properly defining and serving the assessment areas, a bank is also subject to analysis of its loan-to-deposit ratio, its borrower profiles, its investments and services, comments from the community and distribution of its loans, including those for community development purposes.

---

[2] Federal Financial Institutions Examination Council, "Explanation of the Community Reinvestment Act Asset-Size Threshold Change," 2017

[3] Ibid.

Directly below, we summarize some of the CRA issues common amongst our client banks, but later, we will share some of the more innovative and original ideas to have come from them.

CONTRIBUTIONS AND DONATIONS

Many banks don't do a good job in gathering documentation to support that their contributions have a community development purpose. This is often because they simply don't ask. We are frequently asked to review the list of each contribution made to a business, charity or organization, and are provided with no background information on the beneficiary. How are we, or the regulators, to know that a $1,000 check to the "Wine Tasting Ball" didn't just buy alcohol for the la-de-das of the town? Could this contribution, in fact, have supported an event which made considerable donations to the local boys' and girls' club to subsidize a summer camp, which allows both parents to continue working in the community through summer? If so, that additional information supports the community development purpose for sure.

Sponsoring chili cook-offs, golf tournaments and galas are good for business development and name recognition, but, with the right documentation, they can receive credit for their community development purposes as well! One best practice we often recommend is for accounts payable to require the business or organization requesting funds to identify the organization's mission and individual or geographic beneficiaries on the fund request form. Banks would also do well to provide lenders and executive officers with practical examples of income assistance or community development initiatives.

COMMUNITY DEVELOPMENT SERVICES

Similar to the contributions challenge, bank employees are rightfully encouraged to participate in their communities, but some banks don't communicate that a financial component is needed in order to receive CRA credit. Teaching Sunday school or volunteering for school sporting events do not qualify. The message needs to be communicated and incentivized for employees to share their specialized financial knowledge and skills with the community.

Another challenge community banks face, especially those well past *de novo* status, is that the low-hanging fruit is gone when it comes to community development services or lending. In most community banks, each employee is responsible for many different functions; scouring the street for CRA opportunities is sometimes tabled because of other daily, monthly and quarterly deadlines. Community banks don't have the resources that larger institutions have, and so it is likely they don't employ a community development officer whose sole function is to hunt opportunities. Likewise, their assessment areas are only so big, yet these are the areas given the most scrutiny during exams.

We recommend that our clients pair up with a partner to increase their community development opportunities. This goes back to the old adage, "you don't know what you don't know." By teaming up with a local organization, such as Habitat for Humanity for example, opportunities to assist with affordable home construction, neighborhood revitalization and financial education may present themselves in ways banks would otherwise have missed. The same goes for the local United Way chapter, Junior Achievement and other, often smaller local organizations. Simply letting these organizations know that the bank has the resources and willingness is akin to putting yourselves on call for CRA opportunities. Everybody wins.

RESIDENTIAL LENDING

Circling back to the limited size of many community banks' assessment areas, these institutions are challenged to identify qualified LMI borrowers for home loans. But institutions that do cover larger geographies have told us they simply do not have the resources or incentive pay programs to reach affordable housing and LMI borrowers. Carefully arranged, targeted marketing efforts can help in this area, as can the right partnerships – as previously discussed.

SUCCESSES AND INNOVATION

Community banks are achieving great things in small business lending. Responsible for more than 40 percent of the nation's small business lending (despite holding only 13 percent in assets), community banks provide a disproportionately high share of small business credit as compared to large banks. This is important because small businesses (defined here as having less than 500 employees) "provide 50 percent of U.S. private employment."[4] Thus, so long as the economy is relatively healthy, our community banks are succeeding in lending to businesses of all sizes and in all geographies of their community.

We like to ask our banks what they have done to organically support general community development. One of our clients has achieved success through an attorney promotion, in which they not only welcome Interest on Trust Accounts (IOTA), but with each account opened, they donate $250 to the Legal Aid society for the county in which the attorney operates. To make their annual donation dollars go further and create the most positive impact for the community, some institutions have started earmarking a

---

[4] Esther L. George, "Why Community Banks Matter," Remarks at Federal Reserve Bank of New York Community Banking Conference, April 6, 2017, available at https://www.kansascityfed.org/~/media/files/publicat/speeches/2017/2017-george-nyfed-4-6.pdf

percentage of their contribution funds to be used strictly for community development or income assistance.

Recognizing the issue of a growing population of unbanked (person/family without at least one bank account with an insured institution) and underbanked, we have seen a greater willingness by community banks to offer "second chance" accounts for those who have previously been shut off from traditional banking based on poor loan or deposit account activity. The reason for this is most often tied back to relationship banking. Community banks typically operate through a hands-on, personal model. Working closely with their customers, often through generations, they can provide solid financial literacy and independence for those who are willing and ready to proceed down that path.

STORYTELLING MATTERS

The single piece of CRA-related advice that we most often give our clients is to *tell their story.* This is not accomplished by collecting a pile of loose papers and leaving them (or a flash drive) in the conference room with an examiner. Clearly, you want documentation to back up each of your claims, but by using words and emotion, bankers can create a colorful and intricate picture that speaks volumes to the ears and sometimes to the hearts of their examiners. CRA exams are a chance to shine. This is your time; this is your spotlight. Be proud of what you accomplish with often-limited resources, and go out there and start bragging.

KRISTEN STOGNIEW is a shareholder in the Financial Institutions Advisory Group of Saltmarsh, Cleaveland & Gund. She has more than 20 years of experience as a trusted advisor to community banks on legal, operational and compliance concerns. Kristen leads a team of dedicated professionals who provide internal audits, compliance reviews and other consulting services that help clients operate safely, soundly and in compliance with regulatory requirements. Her primary areas of review include BSA, Loan and Deposit Compliance, Marketing and Retail Delivery (including Social Media), Trust, Governance and ACH. She graduated from the University of South Florida with a B.S. in Finance and earned her J.D. from Stetson University College of Law. She is a Certified Fraud Examiner and Member of the Florida Bar Association.

SARAH OLIVER is a consultant in the Financial Institutions Advisory Group of Saltmarsh, Cleaveland & Gund. Her primary areas of expertise include providing compliance review, assisting with special research matters and consulting on deposit and lending related regulations as well as social media approaches for financial institutions. Sarah is a Certified Regulatory Compliance Manager. She actively shares content on Twitter at @sarahbankercrcm and her LinkedIn profile at www.linkedin.com/in/saraholivercrcm.

PERIN BUSH is a Certified Regulatory Compliance Manager and has been a member of the consulting team in Saltmarsh's Financial Institutions Advisory Group since 2012. She has worked in the financial institution industry since 1976, and works extensively with financial institution clients, providing internal audit, loan operations, compliance and other consulting services. She is an active member in the Panhandle Regulatory Compliance Officer Association.

CRA AT FORTY

WHERE WE'RE GOING

IT'S TIME TO GROW UP: STRATEGIES FOR CRA'S NEXT EVOLUTION

Chip Clements
Forcht Bank

The Community Reinvestment Act was created in 1977 and since that time there have been only minor fundamental changes to its design. We've seen amendments allowing regulators to give credit for investments in minority- and women-owned banks; requiring state-by-state   CRA analysis when   conducting   multi-state examinations; and a handful of other updates.

To put 40 years in perspective: Over that time, the world has witnessed roller rinks, disco, floppy disks, Trapper Keepers, heavy metal hair bands, "You've Got Mail," pagers, the Macarena, Gameboys   and   many   more   important and   fundamental advancements and innovations. In the mortgage industry, we saw the rise of non-bank mortgage lenders who exploded with loan growth and then subsequently imploded during a sub-prime and housing crisis. We witnessed economic recessions and stock market crashes. We saw consumer expectations and communication fundamentally changed by the global, immediate connectivity of the Internet. To our regret, we've witnessed a diminishing middle class and widening income inequality coupled with war and terrorism within our borders. Change, resiliency and diversity are common traits of our great nation. These attributes have catapulted us through the past 40 years regardless of what we have faced. But in all that time, our Community Reinvestment Act has languished in the past with a mullet haircut, acid-washed jeans and a Members Only jacket.

This difference has been most evident in the past few years as stagnant wages, rapid home appreciation and lack of affordable housing inventory has made the possibility of homeownership a distant dream for many people. Per Fannie Mae, as of June 2017 only 27 percent of people state that it's a good time to buy a home, a survey low.[1] In addition, the Home Affordability Index has not seen equilibrium with historical averages since 2008.[2] When you take these issues and add in the reality of tighter credit standards, massive student loan debt and diminished federal, state and local subsidy programs, meeting the CRA requirements for lending can prove very difficult for most banks. CRA needs to be brought current to reflect the challenges we experience today and not the world of 40 years ago.

---

[1] Matthew Classick, "A Seller's Market? Consumers Express Diverging Sentiment on Home Buying and Selling May," Fannie Mae, June 7, 2017, available at http://www.fanniemae.com/portal/media/corporate-news/2017/may-home-purchase-sentiment-index-6566.html

[2] ATTOM, "Q2 2017 U.S. Median Home Price at Least Affordable Level Since Q3 2008," June 29, 2017, available at https://www.attomdata.com/news/home-prices-and-sales/q2-2017-home-affordability-index/

Any manufactured home loan originated should receive CRA lending credit regardless of income or census tract.

If you research how many banks and mortgage companies actually lend on manufactured homes you would be shocked at how few accept this property type. For the ones that do lend on manufactured homes, you will typically find stringent credit "overlays" or greater down payment requirements for those borrowers. Those tighter loan standards make manufactured home applicants more difficult to approve than if the exact same borrower wanted to purchase a site-built home.

I have been amazed by how many borrowers, community groups, government housing employees and bank officers actually don't know that Fannie Mae and Freddie Mac will purchase manufactured home loans with only a 5 percent down payment; FHA loans only require 3 percent. The lack of knowledge is not their fault and only proves my point. Many lending institutions require greater down payments and higher credit scores for manufactured homes than what the GSE's and HUD require (e.g. overlays). Subsequently, fewer manufactured home applicants are approved by these institutions for a property type that is usually the most affordable per square foot for rural borrowers.[3] The lack of manufactured home lending by many mortgage companies and banks has allowed two mortgage lenders to dominate this market. Per the Housing Assistance Council, "two large mortgage companies reported 41 percent of all rural manufactured home applications in 2012, neither of which was evaluated under CRA."[4]

---

[3] Smart Growth American, "Rural Development Policy Toolkit: Providing Well-Place Affordable Housing in Rural Communities," April 2017, available at
https://smartgrowthamerica.org/app/uploads/2017/04/rural-toolkit_affordable-housing.pdf

[4] Housing Assistance Council, "CRA in Rural America: The Community Reinvestment Act and Mortgage Lending in Rural Communities," January 2015, available at
http://www.ruralhome.org/storage/documents/publications/rrreports/rrr-cra-in-rural-america.pdf

I have been involved in lending policy for 20 years, and every bank has the right to develop lending policies that are prudent for the safety and soundness of its institution. But refusing or limiting lending on a property type that is a vital source of affordable housing to many rural communities is a concern that needs to be addressed. One way to solve this problem and promote manufactured home lending is to give CRA lending credit specifically for manufactured housing properties regardless of the borrower's income level or the property's census tract. Another alternative would be to segregate this property type into its own specific examination category with definitive metrics by which to gauge bank performance in their respective communities.

Require non-depository mortgage lending institutions to meet certain revised CRA lending requirements in states where they actively lend.

What difference is there between a bank originating mortgage loans versus a non-depository mortgage lender originating them? Absolutely none, so non-depository mortgage lenders should be held accountable to certain LMI lending requirements in the states they "serve." Six out of the top 10 mortgage originators are non-bank mortgage lenders not regulated by CRA.[5] It's time the Community Reinvestment Act evolves to recognize this fact.

If we want to increase lending to LMI borrowers or census tracts, why are we excluding 60 percent of the largest originators from this requirement? A non-depository lender is different from a bank and not all requirements of CRA should apply to them. But revisions to the Act could be made to include certain lending requirements based on peer activity to hold these non-depository institutions accountable to LMI lending expectations.

---

[5] Michele Lerner, "The mortgage market is now dominated by non-bank lenders," The Washington Post, February 23, 2017

Financial and homebuyer education should be a required aspect of the mortgage process and receive CRA credit.

You may passionately disagree with me on this next point, but every person in America should not own a home. Homeownership is not an inherent right but instead a privilege. The financial education and awareness necessary for homeownership is the responsibility of many people and organizations that educate and assist people who want to achieve this. This is no different than a parent, pastor or teacher who educates a young adult on how to achieve their dream of attending college.

Buying a home is the largest financial decision that most people make in their lifetime, but very few people actually understand the responsibilities, requirements and process to accomplish it. When I purchased my first home, I was clueless. There were a myriad of financial questions and I had no idea where to start. Then when I actually bought the home, I didn't realize all of the hard work, time and money needed to own it versus living in an apartment. It took me a week before I realized that I needed to buy a lawn mower to cut the grass. But, like many young adults with little disposable income, I was broke until payday, so the grass was going to have to wait another week.

If we want to empower as many people to own a home as possible, and if we want as many people to be homeowners as possible, we must educate people so they are as equipped as possible for the challenges and responsibilities that will come with it. Who better to educate our communities on responsible banking services then the banks that serve those communities? This is what we do every day. We are the subject matter experts and should take on that role of educator to our communities so they can make safe and sound financial decisions. We need to teach credit responsibility, safe banking practices, home buying, budgeting and many other things to ensure that our clients do not make decisions that could harm them for years to come. We should not limit education to LMI borrowers or census tracts as there are just as many first-time homebuyers at all income levels that don't understand these basic concepts. Anyone who has ever originated a mortgage loan can attest to this.

Increase the CRA-qualifying income limit dramatically or allow CRA lending credit for up to 175 percent of the current Area Median Income level.

In my career, I have developed several lending programs to specifically assist LMI borrowers. It's incredibly frustrating when a community's Area Median Income (AMI) is so low that most applicants will not qualify for a mortgage loan due to their lack of income compared to their existing debt. This disparity is increasingly an issue with borrowers who are LMI.

In my state, there are counties where the AMI is only $34,200. To keep the homebuyer's debt-to-income ratio at 41 percent, their total monthly debt, including their proposed mortgage payment and all other debt payments, must not exceed $1,168. Now, assume the borrower has average monthly expenses and maintains a budget. Like most of us, the borrower likely has a $250 car payment with insurance, $230 for utilities and phone and food and household expenses of $250, bringing those total monthly payments to $730. That leaves the borrower just $430 for a principal and interest monthly mortgage payment.

Let's take a step further. If the borrower is looking to stay on budget, a $430 monthly mortgage payment roughly equates to a home purchase price of $60,000. In most every county in my state, and most state across the nation, finding a home in a safe, desirable neighborhood to raise a family at that price is, at best, difficult. I'll use this opportunity to remind you of the importance of manufactured housing to meet affordable housing needs.

To further complicate this discussion, in many cities such as San Francisco or Washington D.C., home values are rapidly increasing, making it nearly impossible for a borrower at 100 percent of AMI to purchase a home, much less someone at or below 80 percent AMI. In addition, most down payment assistance programs, subsidies or other discounts require borrowers to meet the LMI income level to receive benefit. Those potential homebuyers, who are slightly above the AMI for their community, and also in a somewhat better financial position to purchase a home, are locked out of these programs.

Now, let's quickly adjust this scenario. Looking at the AMI of $34,200, let's say we increase the CRA-qualifying income level to 175 percent of the AMI. This increases the borrower's allowed income maximum to $59,850, opening up access to a higher payment and assistance programs. For perspective, in my state, the average salary for a teacher is $50,000[6], a police officer is $41,300[7] and a firefighter is $41,923.[8]

To summarize, the HUD AMI limits have not increased or equalized with rising prices on consumer goods, stagnant wages and the regular cycles of prosperity and recession that our economy goes through. We must look at the income formula and encompass more people that are in need of mortgage assistance through down payment programs, rate subsidies and specific loan programs tailored to meet the demand.

For the sake of time, I'm only addressing one specific aspect of the Community Reinvestment Act and offering thoughts on the changes needed. Some may view these changes as far-reaching and

---

[6] Teaching Degree.org, available at http://www.teachingdegree.org/kentucky/salary/

[7] Tim Hrenchir, "What Is Average Salary of a Police Officer in Kentucky?" Newsmax.com, August 20, 2015, available at http://www.newsmax.com/FastFeatures/average-salary-police-officer-kentucky/2015/08/20/id/671085/

[8] Salary.com, available at http://www1.salary.com/KY/Fire-Fighter-salary.html

excessively burdensome. However, if you take a look at each suggestion carefully, you will find one common thread among all of them – a focus on inclusion and acceptance in order to assist more people in need.

Our desire should be to place more potential homebuyers under CRA regulatory requirements and provide more assistance, more education and more opportunities. As community bankers, we have the duty to serve those communities that have placed their trust in us and the vast majority of us are willing and able. I'm not proposing more regulation with my suggestions. I'm simply asking that we utilize the wisdom and knowledge that comes with growing older and expand the reach of the Community Reinvestment Act so we may serve more people tomorrow than we have today.

CHIP CLEMENTS joined Forcht Bank in August 2015 as Executive Vice President of Mortgage Lending & Servicing. Prior to that role, he held similar positions at Republic Bank & Trust and New Equity Mortgage. Mr. Clements has created or turned around various bank divisions including mortgage lending, consumer lending, credit cards, indirect auto, online lending, mortgage correspondent lending, information technology security, enterprise risk management and loan servicing. He has also been heavily involved in mergers and acquisitions of FDIC failed banks. He can be reached for further comment at chipclements.me@gmail.com.

LEVERAGING FACTORY-BUILT PROCESSES TO MAKE HOMES AFFORDABLE

Stacey Epperson
Next Step Network

We are approaching the zenith of a housing affordability crisis. As home prices continue to rise, housing stock shrinks and wages remain stagnant, Americans increasingly find themselves unable to secure sustainable housing. Factory-built housing presents a viable solution for affordable and sustainable homeownership, and the tools and regulations provided by the Community Reinvestment Act are an invaluable asset for increasing access to factory-built homes.

For much of modern American history, homeownership has been judged as an indicator of success. Ask an individual if they have aspirations to own a home someday, and most would say yes.

Attitudes and ideologies shift and change over time, but homeownership has remained an intractable part of achieving the oft-sought "American Dream."

But what happens when this benchmark is placed further and further out of reach? What is the impact on not only individuals and families, but on whole communities? How do we reconcile this vision – each person with the opportunity to own his or her own home – with a reality that is evaporating before our eyes?

These aren't just hypothetical questions, but rather ones to which communities across the country are scrambling to find answers. The U.S. homeownership rate is at its lowest point in decades, falling to just 63.7 percent.[1] This drop has been attributed to a number of factors, but one prevailing issue is a pervasive lack of affordable housing options for low- and moderate-income individuals and families. As of June 2017, the median price for a new single-family home in the U.S. was $310,800[2] – and wages are not rising commensurately with increased market prices.

But the national numbers fail to paint a picture of the depth of this housing crisis in many communities. Real estate marketplace giant Trulia shows that nationwide, the number of "starter homes" available – smaller, more affordable homes – has dropped 40 percent since 2012. In cities like Austin and San Antonio, Texas, more than 80 percent of this housing stock has disappeared.[3]

---

[1] U.S. Census Bureau, "Quarterly Residential Vacancies and Homeownership, Second Quarter 2017," Release Number BC17-110, July 27, 2017, available at https://www.census.gov/housing/hvs/files/ currenthvspress.pdf

[2] U.S. Census Bureau, "Median and Average Sales Prices of New Homes Sold in United States," June 2017, available at https://www.census.gov/construction/hrs/pdf/uspricemon.pdf

[3] Patrick Sisson, "Starter Home Inventory Drop Burdens First-Time Buyers, Report Revels," Curbed, March 21, 2016, available at https://www.curbed.com/2016/3/21/11273004/buying-homes-major-cities-unaffordable-inventory-starter-homes

People aren't just being priced out of the single-family home market. According to the Joint Center for Housing Studies at Harvard University, modestly priced rental housing is also disappearing: "Between 2005 and 2015, the number of rental units costing less than $800 per month declined while the number costing over $2,000 per month jumped by 1.5 million."[4] Of U.S. renters, 11 million are classified as severely cost-burdened, spending more than 50 percent of their income on housing costs.[5] The impact of increased housing costs crosses the urban and rural divide, affecting communities from coast to coast. The National Low Income Housing Center estimates that in order to afford a modest, two-bedroom rental home in the U.S., renters need to make $21.21 per hour – $13.96 higher than the federal minimum wage.[6]

Those looking to the federal government for solutions are unlikely to find remedy. The Trump administration's proposed budget for fiscal year 2018 takes a particularly harsh swipe at funding for programs that encourage affordable housing and community development. Programs within USDA's Rural Development office face crippling budget cuts or outright elimination – like the Mutual Self-Help Housing program and the Section 502 direct loan program that have helped so many rural Americans purchase their own homes. The budget completely eliminates Community Development Block Grant funds (CDBG) and the HOME Investment Partnerships Program administered by the Department of Housing and Community Development.[7]

---

[4] Joint Center for Housing Studies of Harvard University, "The State of the Nation's Housing 2017," June 16, 2017, available at http://www.jchs.harvard.edu/research/publications/state-nations-housing-2017.

[5] Ibid.

[6] National Low Income Housing Coalition, "Out of Reach 2017 The High Cost of Housing," June 2017, available at http://nlihc.org/sites/default/files/oor/OOR_2017.pdf

[7] Stacey Epperson, "What Does the Trump Agenda Mean for Manufactured Housing?," June 21, 2017, available at http://www/nextstepus.org/news/?p=2329

In lieu of focused, national polices geared toward expanding affordable homeownership, local leaders and advocates will need to be creative and open-minded in crafting affordable housing solutions that increase homeownership opportunities for individuals and families.

As it stands today, manufactured housing is the largest source of unsubsidized, affordable housing stock, with about 6.8 million occupied homes in the country. Manufactured homes make up about 6 percent of the national housing stock, and are an indispensable source of housing in many communities. In 2015, the average sales price of a new manufactured home was $68,000 – compared to $360,600 for a new, single-family site-built home.[8] This dramatic difference in cost opens up the chance to own a home to a greatly expanded pool of individuals and families.

It's an affordable solution sitting right in front of many local and community leaders, and yet one that is often overlooked. In fact, factory-built housing typically faces opposition from communities. A lack of clear and consistent zoning regulations adversely impacts the expanded use of these homes. They are often the target of NIMBY-ism ("Not in My Backyard") – the misconception from residents being that expanded use of factory-built homes would have a detrimental impact in their community. Local lenders and home appraisers lack knowledge about factory-built homes, making it more difficult for prospective homebuyers to secure sound financing.

Many of these challenges facing factory-built housing are steeped in outdated stereotypes, misinformation and decades of negative portrayal in popular culture. It starts with outmoded terminology. When referencing this housing stock, many use terms like "mobile

---

[8] Lance George, "Manufactured Housing," 2016 Advocates' Guide: An Educational Primer on Federal Programs and Resources Related to Affordable Housing and Community Development, available at http://nlihc.org/sites/default/files/2016_Advocates-Guide.pdf

home" or "trailer." While "trailer" is more a derogatory term – one that is also offensive to the millions of families all over the country who live in these homes – mobile home is actually a categorically incorrect definition (unless one is referring to a home constructed prior to 1976). That year, the Department of Housing and Urban Development enacted the Manufactured Home Construction and Safety Standards, also known as the HUD Code, creating a national blueprint for the design, performance and installation of all manufactured homes in the country.

Today's manufactured housing stock is a far cry from the popular perception that is still a part of our cultural zeitgeist. The HUD Code has been updated and amended to include much-improved energy efficiency standards. In 2005, HUD issued the Model Manufactured Home Installation Standards, outlining methods for on-site installation that comply with the HUD Code. Improved building technology, manufacturing processes and regulatory mechanisms have combined to create a vastly different landscape for factory-built housing.

Modern manufactured and modular homes also present many advantages for the buyer. The construction of a factory-built home is process-based, so building times are more predictable and the controlled environment prevents damage or loss due to weather and theft. Customization can also be more controlled, with specific costs tied to features and amenities up front.

Home manufacturing facilities are also making great strides in reducing waste in building practices. Recently, all 36 of the manufacturing facilities owned and operated by Clayton Homes – one of the nation's largest manufactured and modular homebuilders – were awarded an ISO 14001 registration, a set of internationally agreed-upon measures that are designed to reduce the cost of waste management and reduce energy consumption.[9]

Manufacturers are also building more energy-efficient homes, generating less impact on the environment and saving families hundreds of dollars in monthly utility bills.

Even when considering these positive traits of factory-built housing, there is much work to be done so that communities can fully leverage these homes for increased affordable homeownership opportunities.

One key area of this space that needs the thought leadership of myriad stakeholders dedicated to expanding the use of factory-built housing is lending and finance. Currently, chattel – or personal property loans – dominate the manufactured housing market. These higher-touch, lower-volume loans are characterized by high interest rates and shorter loan terms. Next Step – as a part of our SmartMH program – is working with Freddie Mac to expand the number of lenders that originate real property loans on ENERGY STAR® manufactured homes, allowing greater access to more lenders and fair lending products. We are also using homebuyer education specific to factory-built housing and housing counseling to educate prospective homebuyers about making smart, sustainable financing decisions.

SmartMH is a direct market intervention, dedicated to expanding mortgage capital for manufactured homes, while creating better educated and prepared homebuyers. We're taking individuals who may be currently unable to purchase a home – due to credit history, lack of down payment or other factors – and making them "mortgage ready" buyers.

The Community Reinvestment Act offers a valuable tool for increased mortgage lending on manufactured homes. Banks and lending institutions have the opportunity to earn CRA credit for

---

[9] Jennifer Goodman, "Clayton Ups Its Green Game," Builder Magazine, November 2, 2016, available at http://www.builderonline.com/building/building-science/clayton-ups-its-green-game_o.

manufactured home lending. Manufactured homes represent the largest source of unsubsidized affordable housing, and many of the manufactured homebuyers are low- to moderate-income individuals and families in rural communities. More development projects are also leveraging factory-built homes for infill opportunities in cities, contributing to neighborhood and community revitalization efforts.

Nonprofit housing organizations have been leading the way in incorporating factory-built housing solutions into communities. Next Step serves to work collaboratively with these organizations, providing technical expertise in the manufactured housing space and acting as an intermediary between manufacturers, retail home centers and lenders. To date, Next Step network members have placed 463 new ENERGY STAR® factory-built homes, contributing to more than $4 million in 30-year energy cost savings for homeowners and families.

In order to foster factory-built housing as an affordable option for communities, there needs to be continued collaboration among key stakeholders, further advancements in manufacturing and building technology and innovative lending products and practices that bolster lending to create an enhanced space for manufactured housing. Through these collaborations, we can increase the access to opportunity for families to achieve the dream of homeownership, wealth building and prosperity.

STACEY EPPERSON is a native of rural Kentucky and has worked in affordable housing throughout her entire career. In 2010, after nine years as President & CEO of Frontier Housing in northeastern Kentucky, Stacey assumed leadership of Next Step. In 2012, Stacey was elected an Ashoka Fellow for her innovative approach to creating the only independent distribution channel for affordable manufactured housing. She was recognized as one of CFED's Innovators-in-Residence and has completed the Achieving Excellence in Community Development Program at Harvard's JFK School of Government. Stacey holds a Masters of Public Administration from Western Kentucky University, and attended the University of Kentucky Patterson School of Diplomacy and International Commerce. Stacey serves on the Freddie Mac Affordable Housing Advisory Council.

URBAN ACUPUNCTURE: A SOLUTION FOR VACANT AND ABANDONED PROPERTIES

Gill Holland
Portland Investment Initiative[1]

Throughout the United States and all of its great cities, if you drive through certain neighborhoods, you can't help but notice the huge number of decaying, vacant and abandoned properties. In my hometown of Louisville, Kentucky, there are nine neighborhoods "West of 9th Street" that fall into this category.

We need to come together as fellow Americans nationally, and locally as neighbors, and remedy this blight, because the decay can't be missed and should no longer be ignored. While certain publications like the Courier-Journal of Kentucky, whose writer Joe Gerth addressed the problem in a recent column "Scourge of

---

[1] A version of this article first appeared in Louisville's Courier-Journal on May 16, 2017 and has been included here with the author's and newspaper's permission.

vacant homes killing West Louisville,"[2] are addressing the issue, the reality is many of these neighborhoods are not visited by the more affluent and politically-connected citizens who could help make a change.

As the nation talks about aging infrastructure and needed investment, vacant and abandoned properties should be part of that discussion. Spending $10 billion on highways and bridges is one thing and spending that same amount in $100,000 investments in 100,000 places is another that would also have huge impact. The issue of vacant and abandoned properties is one of Louisville's greatest challenges – and I believe one of the great opportunities for all American cities. My team has been working in one of the nine neighborhoods "West of 9th Street" – the historic Portland neighborhood – for the last four years focused on exactly this issue of "vacant, abandoned properties" (VAPs).

Using "urban acupuncture," we try to acquire the worst vacant house on each block and renovate it. This takes away the negative ripple effect of a VAP and replaces it with a much-needed affordable housing opportunity. For most folks, the common question is whether to buy the "worst house on the best block or the best house on the worse block," so we buy the worst house on the worst block. I hope my insights can help policymakers, bankers, developers and nonprofit service providers brainstorm some potential out-of-the-box market-based solutions.

The discriminatory practice of redlining has been against the law for decades, and in 1977 the Community Reinvestment Act was passed to address redlining and encourage banks to lend in economically-challenged areas. Some local banks do more than just check the box when it comes to their CRA compliance;

---

[2] Joseph Gerth, "Scourge of vacant homes killing western Louisville," USA Today, March 25, 2017, available at https://www.usatoday.com/story/news/local/joseph-gerth/2017/03/25/scourge-vacant-homes-killing-western-louisville-joseph-gerth/99535416/

however, the vast majority of America's challenged neighborhoods are still dealing with the real-world consequences of the legacy of redlining.

In Louisville, most of the crumbling structures (VAPs) can be acquired for under $10,000. That is the cash cost, and does not take into account the time often spent tracking down who legally owns the property as well as dealing with city, state and third party lien-holders. Our redevelopment company's average renovation cost is $70,000, and our total cash investment averages $80,000 per house. The market distortion which then leads to what is today effectively an "economic (not overtly racial) redlining" occurs when we finish one of these lovely historic houses, but both the banks and the Jefferson County Property Valuation Administrator say the house is "worth" about $28,000 based on "area comparisons" included in required appraisals. It is virtually impossible to get any mortgage, construction loan or even home improvement loan on these houses since the amount required to renovate is so much more than what the finished "value" will be.

The reason for this disparity is simple and makes sense at first blush – banks rely on appraisals that use "area comparisons" when they decide how much to lend. Decades of disinvestment, coupled with white flight, the move to the suburbs after the interstate highways were built and the city's documented history of redlining[3] have made it difficult, if not impossible, for certain groups to build equity through their homes over the last three generations. Subsequent vicious cycles of crime, under-employment and drug abuse have led to one in four area properties being VAP in distressed neighborhoods, so the continual $10,000 "sales comps" preclude any other type of market-based valuation. It is an "apples to oranges" comparison,

[3] Eric Bosco, "Map of the Month: Redlining Louisville: The History of Race, Class, and Real Estate," Data-Smart City Solutions, June 15, 2017, available at http://datasmart.ash.harvard.edu/news/article/map-of-the-month-redlining-louisville-1062

since the perfectly nice houses in these areas are being lumped in with VAPs, and the comparisons are inherently unfair.

This all gives us an opportunity to discuss how we could help the banks in our area unite for the greater good. If every bank in the nation would publicly commit to attaining an outstanding on their Community Reinvestment Act (CRA) Report, we could better finance housing for more of our neighbors in need. If banks would innovate and be flexible in their methodology to appraise rehabilitated VAPs, they could support a much different result.

There are 30,000 families on the affordable housing wait list in Jefferson County, where the city of Louisville is located. Affordable housing for a family of four in our area is about $730 per month. We charge $650 a month to rent one of our rehabilitated houses. An appraisal based on this monthly rent (or "cap-rate" for industry professionals) would suggest our newly renovated house should be worth over $90,000.

There are close to 8,000 VAPs in Louisville; about 5,800 of those are vacant structures. Using our average figure of $80,000 per residence, our community needs a total of $640 million to renovate every single blighted property. There is a number that each city in America could come up with based on that formula.

The benefits to historically marginalized communities, local families and every American city, including Louisville, would be massive. When a property is left to deteriorate, cities spend about $10,000 for each demolition plus the ongoing yearly maintenance of empty lots. In Louisville alone, that equals $80 million in taxpayer benefit if we actually took care of each vacant property.

Studies show that more jobs are created renovating existing structures than building new ones, because more money goes into labor and less into materials. Another value in renovation is the rebuilding of the cultural identity of an area (many of these challenged neighborhoods are historic) and curing the blight. Renovating is a greater benefit to an area than new construction on an empty lot, since the empty lots don't have as negative a ripple effect as a VAP. In a conversation with a local police officer recently, he shared that police officers are more concerned about being shot answering calls in empty buildings than on empty lots. The negative impact on young children walking past VAP's on the way to and from school contributes to the sense that their neighborhoods – and, by extensions, themselves – have been forgotten. Since fixing up empty buildings displaces no one, this solution doesn't exacerbate gentrification. There could be a moratorium on property tax increases for long-term anchor homeowners to protect their interests.

Based on the 2007 National Association of Home Builders or the 2009 Housing Alliance of Pennsylvania studies, each 100 units of affordable housing – totaling about $10 million of expenditure – creates about 150 jobs in the first year and 40 recurring jobs[4]. Expanding on that, 8,000 units in Louisville would create 12,000 jobs in year one and 3,200 permanent jobs.

An added bonus in Louisville is that the Water Company and Metropolitan Sewer District are publicly owned, and the infrastructure for those city utilities already exists in the challenged areas. Because we as taxpayers have already invested millions of dollars to provide water and sewage services to VAPs, having customers living on restored properties would generate significant revenue. While having citizen-owned utilities may be unique to Louisville and certain other cities, the areas where VAPs are

---

[4] "Financing Affordable Rental Development: Jobs Created by New Construction and Rehabilitation," February 25, 2011, available at http://www.floridahousing.org/FH-ImageWebDocs/UniversalApps/2011/ImportantAnnouncements/012-FinancingAffordableRentaDevelopment/Jobs%20from%20Rental%20Development%20with%20Table%202%2015%202011%20PUBLIC%20DRAFT.pdf

prevalent in all cities are already on the grid in terms of these services.

If we take away the cancerous VAPs and replace them with newly renovated affordable houses, entire neighborhoods will be uplifted. The market will reflect that with a significant increase in property values throughout American cities, not to mention the increase in retail that will come with more "rooftops."

While there are obviously huge economic benefits from more people with homes, imagine the future earnings and benefits that would accrue from safely and securely housing today the many children in America who each year experience some form of homelessness. In Louisville alone, there are 8,000 children in Jefferson County Public Schools who do.

How can we as a nation figure out a way to stimulate the investment needed for affordable housing in our communities? In Louisville, we are pitching a super tax increment financing district (TIF) covering all of the area "West of 9th" and challenging the banks to have the private sector fund a $640 million Community Impact Bond. Our back-of-the-envelope economic impact study based on our returns for investors suggests a healthy return (higher than municipal bonds presently) for the private sector if such a bond could be institutionalized.

Our challenge to the country is to brainstorm a way to find the political will, the private sector capital or a potential for a public-private partnership and the social conscience to house our neighbors, create thousands of good jobs, reduce our crime and homicide rates and rebuild our cities.

GILL HOLLAND lives with his wife and three children in Louisville, where he is a community builder and real estate developer working in the NuLu and historic Portland neighborhoods. He also produces movies, books and music.

A COMMUNITY OF STAKEHOLDERS: THE NEXT 40 YEARS

Claire Raley
BankUnited[1]

The 40th anniversary of the Community Reinvestment Act presents the opportunity to reflect on both the evolution and devolution of the community development paradigm over the last four decades.

This reflection is particularly timely given economic indicators that show continued recovery from the Great Recession through falling unemployment rates and increased business and economic growth, while at the same time many individuals and families struggle to make ends meet. Decreased unemployment and increased GDP has not translated into the increased wage levels necessary to keep

---

[1] The views and opinions expressed in this article are those of the author and do not necessarily reflect the official position or views of BankUnited, N.A., the author's employer.

pace with the costs for basic needs such as housing, food, medical care and transportation. Among these costs, affordability of housing has become the number one issue in many communities across the country. The growing economic disparity between the "haves" and the "have-nots," coupled with increased uncertainty in funding from the Federal government for community development programs, signals an urgent need to reimagine the community development paradigm we have become accustomed to over the past 40 years. Community development practitioners, in partnership with the private, nonprofit and public sectors and community leaders, must develop a new community development paradigm that incorporates changing roles and strategies to address persistent poverty and economic inequality.

During the 40 years since the enactment of CRA, which happens to coincide with my start as a community development practitioner in a municipality in South Florida, the public sector has played a key role in setting policy and providing funding to address community development needs in low-income communities. While many states and local communities have developed their own programs that help to address community needs, the Federal government has significantly influenced the community development paradigm through enactment of key pieces of legislation that provide regulatory mechanisms, valuable grants and subsidy dollars and tax credit incentives in support of community development activities. Included on this list is the enactment of CRA in 1977. It established regulations for ensuring that banks and financial institutions reinvested in all communities within their markets. It created a private source of capital for community development programs and initiatives.

While a review of all federal community development programs could fill volumes, there are four programs that have been particularly important in shaping the current community development landscape. These programs include the Community

Development Block Grant Program[2], which allocates funding to state and local government through a formula based on population, poverty and various housing factors. They also include two key tax credit programs: the Low-Income Housing Tax Credit Program[3], which creates affordable housing; and the New Markets Tax Credit Program[4], which supports low-income, distressed communities through job creation and small business expansion. Finally, the HOME Investment Partnership Program[5] focuses on expanding the capacity of nonprofit organizations to support affordable housing. Under the current proposed Federal budget, many of these programs are slated for reduction, or outright elimination, which will have serious implications for low-income individuals, families and local communities.

---

[2]Community Development Block Grant (CDBG) Program – Title I of the Housing and Community Development Act of 1974 created the Community Development Block Grant (CDBG) Program. The legislation's merging of seven individual competitive grant programs into a "block grant" coupled with providing local communities with the flexibility to determine how funding would be used to meet community needs, was a departure from previous Federal funding through the Department of Housing and Urban Development. CDBG funds are allocated to state and local governments through a formula based on population, poverty and various housing factors.

[3] Low-Income Housing Tax Credit (LIHTC) Program - In 1986, Section 42 of the Internal Revenue Service Code was amended to add the Low-Income Housing Tax Credit (LIHTC). The program creates affordable housing by providing tax credits to property owners who create and maintain affordable housing. The credits are provided for rental units that are offered at rents that are lower than market rates.

[4] New Markets Tax Credit (NMTC) Program – The New Market Tax Credit was enacted by Congress as part of the Community Renewal Tax Relief Act of 2000, added as Section 45D of the Internal Revenue Code. The NMTC provides tax credits for individuals and corporations for making Qualified Equity Investments (QEIs) in Qualified Community Development Entities (CED). The program is targeted to low-income, distressed communities, leveraging private capital in support of job creation and small business expansion.

[5] HOME Investment Partnership Program (HOME) - Created by the Cranston-Gonzalez National Affordable Housing Act of 1990, this program, like CDBG, is allocated to state and local governments as "block grants" on a formula basis. HOME is designed to focus exclusively on affordable housing, including rental, homeownership, new construction and rehabilitation. In an effort to expand the capacity of nonprofit organizations to provide housing, the program specifically spells out that 15 percent of the funding was to go to Community Housing Development Organizations (CHDOs).

The public sector at the local level has traditionally been the nexus point for community development funding, programs and policy. The top-down approach that was used in earlier decades has been replaced by an evolving model for addressing community needs through collaboration with resident stakeholders in low-income communities, along with partners from the nonprofit and for-profit sectors. No one is better than resident stakeholders for giving voice to the needs in the very communities that the community development paradigm seeks to address. We wring our hands over a lack of civic engagement, particularly in the broader context of poor voter turnout for so many local elections where decisions directly impact the everyday life of all residents. But what are we doing to encourage and support increased civic engagement, discussion and discourse? In an increasingly polarized and toxic environment we do not talk, but scream. Instead of listening, we just walk away. We can change this dynamic by building individual and community leadership and shared civic responsibility and accountability across all communities.

Building and supporting a thriving mission-focused nonprofit community development sector is a critical element to the community development paradigm. Capacity building resources and unrestricted core operating support are essential components to building this sector. These resources need to be at levels that are meaningful and available on a multi-year basis. The absence of this sector in a community means that the community development paradigm in that community is incomplete.

For-profit sector partners in the community development paradigm are not just banks and financial institutions; all businesses and corporations are part of the community of stakeholders. All segments of the for-profit sector derive benefit from the communities where they are located. This imparts on them a responsibility to support opportunities for economic prosperity for everyone in the community.

While the need to reimagine the community development paradigm existed well before the Great Recession, there is long lasting fallout from the recession that makes change essential. The recession has had a lasting impact on the public sector, with the fallout continuing to unfold nearly 10 years later. While the greatest uncertainty lies presently at the federal level, this uncertainty has a rippling effect at the state and local level where significant changes have already occurred. Unlike the Federal government that can "just print more money," most state and local governments must annually produce balanced budgets. During the recession, the massive loss of tax revenue by state and local governments meant balancing budgets through cuts to staffing, as well as consolidation or elimination of programs and services, including those that supported community development activities. Unlike many businesses and nonprofit organizations that simply ceased to exist as a result of the recession, state and local governments could not just shut down, though the recession forced some local governments to reduce their hours of operation to three or four days a week. Nearly ten years after the Great Recession, as federal government support has continued to decrease, local and state governments have stayed leaner than pre-recession. It is argued by some that the reduction in the size of government is good. However, the need for community development programs and services has not lessened.

In this new community development paradigm where government is leaner, community needs continue to grow and somehow seem more complicated. Who fills the community development gaps? The short answer is everyone. In the new community development paradigm, we must achieve a heightened level of community development self-sufficiency at the local level. This means that all stakeholders must sit at the same table, roll up their sleeves, lock arms and collectively find lasting solutions for ending persistent poverty and economic inequality. Working in silos has not and does not work – no one community stakeholder has greater responsibility or ownership than another. Businesses, corporations, nonprofit organizations, residents, civic organizations, government, hospitals, colleges, foundations, philanthropies and faith-based organizations are all members of the stakeholder community. A realignment of stakeholder roles, responsibilities and the identification of clearly defined priorities is essential. It will take leadership, commitment, vision, risk, respect and trust in order to build a new community development paradigm that results in real and lasting change and long-term solutions.

CLAIRE RALEY is SVP, Community Development Officer with BankUnited. In this position she oversees, coordinates and provides strategic direction for the bank's CRA and community development initiatives in Florida and New York. Prior to BankUnited, Ms. Raley worked in community development with other banks, including Chase and Washington Mutual, as well as government agencies and nonprofit organizations. Her expertise includes the Community Reinvestment Act, corporate community affairs, philanthropy and social responsibility and community and affordable housing development. Ms. Raley holds a B.S. from Florida State University and a Masters of Public Administration from Florida International University. She serves on the Board of Directors of Florida Community Loan Fund, Neighborhood Lending Partners and Catalyst Miami.

HEALTHY COMMUNITIES: THINKING BEYOND THE HOUSING BOX TO COMMUNITIES OF CHOICE

Ian Nunley & Nidia Logan-Robinson
Innovate Memphis

The federal Community Reinvestment Act was created in 1977 as a direct response to rampant redlining across the United States that systematically denied home loans and financial investment in select neighborhoods based on race or ethnic composition. The birth of the CRA rightfully shaped the pattern of investment that followed, with a significant majority of CRA-qualifying bank activities in low- to moderate-income neighborhoods focusing on affordable housing development, direct home loans and credit counseling. But housing alone is not the only form of asset building needed to drive increased equity for our distressed neighborhoods. At Innovate Memphis, we believe that impactful investment needs to extend beyond housing to truly change a community.

INVESTIGATE THE CHALLENGE

Truly achieving "innovativeness" in the application of the CRA should deliver new financial tools and increase the impact of dollars spent. To this end, banks, federal regulators, community development corporations (CDCs), local government and philanthropy all must play an active and collaborative role in identifying the true needs of residents in LMI neighborhoods in order to build a strategic vision for more equitable empowerment. Building these associations not only helps stakeholders better identify and understand local needs, but also draws upon a more robust toolkit of lending and investment products that can help remedy those needs. Practitioners should also look to the policies, programs and initiatives of peer cities for inspiration and promising practices to address common challenges. Cultivating healthier communities will require more creativity and flexibility in identifying the activities that successfully meet local community development needs while qualifying for CRA credit.

While the pronounced emphasis on housing provides significant benefits in communities of need, it is merely one piece of the puzzle in creating more holistic "healthy communities" that provide access to choices that empower residents economically, socially and environmentally. Healthy communities include housing choice, but also strong small business activity, access to quality schools and green space, reliable internet connectivity, building weatherization and much more. In 2014, the Federal Reserve Bank of Dallas supported this idea in a white paper entitled, "Healthy Communities: A Framework for Meeting CRA Obligations," which outlined a detailed and comprehensive checklist for holistic community development that fits within the parameters of the CRA.[1] The Healthy Communities Framework includes a series of best practices for model community development[2]:

- Use innovative methods to leverage private capital;
- Blend people and place-based strategies to realize a broader vision;
- Provide equal opportunity access to quality education so that everyone can reach their highest potential;
- Measure outcomes to identify what works; and
- Invest resources in what works.

GENERATE NEW IDEAS

The push for greater innovation requires buy-in and cooperation between all stakeholders involved in community building. Financers, regulators, builders and philanthropies all must work together to create a progressive climate that opens up new arenas for accessing and applying capital. While affordable housing is essential, targeted infrastructure investments that expand transit access, small business development and land use changes can help provide additional support to create healthier, more sustainable communities.

Bank CRA officers can further promote innovative approaches in community development by expressly pushing for deals that move beyond housing in ways that both impact neighborhoods and best fit with their institutions' missions. Layered projects, such as mixed-use or transit-oriented developments, offer the opportunity to improve local access to both housing and commercial prospects. Banks can use the strategic planning process afforded

---

[1] "Healthy Communities: A Framework for Meeting CRA Obligations" by Elizabeth Sobel Blum, Federal Reserve Bank of Dallas, March 2014.

[2] Ibid, page 3.

by the CRA to significantly engage constituencies in local assessment areas. Residents themselves can best speak to neighborhood needs. Incorporating local knowledge into the planning process can help better align need with opportunity and further empower CRA officers to seek out creative deals that are a good fit for the area.

Simultaneously, the regulatory agencies that oversee CRA examinations should accelerate practices that allow banks credit for new, creative projects and lending and investment tools, while keeping a keen eye on safety and soundness. Banks are risk averse in application of the CRA, often defaulting to easily approved projects like affordable housing development to make the process as streamlined as possible. Examiners can expand the types of projects and opportunities that they deem credit-worthy and should make these projects just as easy to pursue. Creating a universal standard of CRA examination qualifications and rating criteria would also help eliminate some of the ambiguity in allowable project types and tools. By reducing barriers and creating a more even playing field among investment and lending opportunities, regulatory agencies establish a fertile environment where banks and community development agencies can innovate and grow their impact.

At the local level, local government, CDCs and philanthropy can all work cooperatively to help cultivate a community development climate that affords some risk to achieve impactful innovation in the policies and programs that uplift healthy communities of choice. The most successful private companies are those that commit to a deliberate process of engagement, research and exploration in order to understand the true desires of their customers and develop products that provide solutions. Shouldn't we want our local community development stakeholders to think along the same lines?

Memphis remains largely divided across economic and racial lines. A recent study found that in 2012, approximately 56 percent of businesses in the city were Black-owned but only collected 0.83 percent of total business revenue.[3] The most economically distressed census tracts are concentrated in a curved fashion both north and south of the central downtown core, creating what is locally referred to as "The C of Poverty." However, local stakeholders are moving to place a more pronounced emphasis on economic empowerment and small business assistance to create a more equitable landscape across Memphis. Preparing to deliver healthy communities of choice requires a deliberate process aimed at LMI residents and neighborhoods, defined targets for improving economic equity, and an effective strategy for communicating with all relevant stakeholders.

The South City Renewal Plan, the targeted redevelopment of a disinvested area on the southern border of the city, serves as a shining example of the type of holistic development projects that can spur communities of choice with CRA-qualifying investible elements. Located just southeast of Memphis' downtown, the initiative includes the historic demolition and replacement of Foote Homes, the city's largest and oldest public housing tract. The Memphis Housing Authority and Division of Housing and Community Development received a Choice Neighborhood Grant from the United States Office of Housing and Urban Development (HUD) for approximately $30 million of the $100 million project.[4] The remaining $70 million will be leveraged from a mix of public and private funding sources.

---

[3] Madeline Faber, "Black-Owned Business Revenue Drops in Memphis", Memphis Daily News, January 29, 2016, available at https://www.memphisdailynews.com/news/2016/jan/29/black-owned-business-revenue-drops/

[4] Bill Dries, "Memphis Nabs $30 Million South City Grant After Last-Minute Negotiations", Memphis Daily News, September 25, 2015, available at https://www.memphisdailynews.com/news/2015/sep/25/choice-neighborhoods-announcement-

The South City Renewal Plan includes elements beyond housing and is aimed at increasing viable commercial activity and improving local access to living wage jobs, public transit, education and quality food.[5] In addition to 712 new units of mixed-income, mixed-use housing, the project aims to expand economic opportunity with ground-floor retail in new mixed-use developments and a commercial exterior repair grant program designed to help make high-quality improvements to existing businesses. Empowering the residents of South City also includes improving access to vital social services. The plan includes improving access to quality food with a new neighborhood grocer and youth and family services with the inclusion of an early childhood development center. Each of these components provides amenities that help uplift the South City neighborhood and increase accessibility to vital community services and opportunity, in effect creating a healthy community.

DELIVER AND ADAPT

As innovative approaches are deployed, we must also take stock of the results of the community development projects and evaluate if investments are truly meeting community needs. In Memphis, we are seeing firsthand how holistic community development projects such as the South City Renewal Plan can be a catalyst not just for providing affordable homes in our LMI neighborhoods, but for opportunities for economic and social empowerment.

For decades, the majority of CRA-qualifying bank activities have focused on housing, and for good reason. Increasing the availability of affordable housing, credit counseling and

---

clouded-by-lipscomb-investigation/

[5] Memphis Housing Authority, "South City Urban Renewal Plan," 2016, available at http://memphisha.org/images/SCURP_DRAFT_MA%20Updates419.pdf

rehabilitation loans help to improve a vital component of livability. But healthy neighborhoods are not solely defined by the local housing stock. In order to truly uplift our LMI communities, stakeholders must work cooperatively to identify tools, projects and products that uplift economic, social and environmental well-being. From banks to regulators, local government and CDCs, everyone involved should allow for flexibility in innovation to help turn our traditionally marginalized communities into thriving ones.

IAN NUNLEY is a Project Manager at Innovate Memphis where he specializes in community development, blight remediation and sustainable materials management. A native of Los Angeles, he recently relocated to Memphis after five years attending graduate school and working as a public policy consultant in the Pacific Northwest. He holds a Bachelor of Arts from Occidental College in Los Angeles and a Masters of Urban Planning and Design from the University of Washington.

NIDIA LOGAN-ROBINSON works for Innovate Memphis, a civic leader in creating groundbreaking public-private partnerships and social innovations to address some of Memphis' most pressing challenges. Her work includes public and nonprofit organization capacity building, developing bold ideas for enhancing community development investments and improving public-sector health and service delivery. She earned a Bachelor of Arts from Hendrix College in Conway, Arkansas and earned a Masters of Public Administration at the University of Memphis. Nidia is a native Arkansan.

REVITALIZING HEALTH: INVESTING IN COMMUNITY WELL-BEING

Ariel Arthur
Kentucky Department of Public Health

MENTAL AND PHYSICAL WELL-BEING

The public health field in the United States has made great strides in the last 20 years. Researchers have begun to understand the relationship between adverse childhood experiences (ACEs) and adult health outcomes. Additional newborn screenings have improved outcomes for infants. Rates of tobacco use have significantly declined and cancer screening rates have increased. Many other milestones have been reached that have positively impacted all of society. Yet significant challenges remain.

Though the United States has secured footing as a leader in technological and medical innovations, the overall health status of its residents lags far behind that of peer nations. Among 35 developed and developing nations throughout the world, the U.S. ranks 26th for life expectancy.[1] Many resources have been dedicated to improving health outcomes by focusing on healthcare, despite the fact that by most estimates, it accounts for less than 10 percent of overall health status.[2] These investments have not resulted in healthy communities; life expectancy in the United States declined in 2015 for the first time since 1993.[3]

COMMUNITY HEALTH

Social factors play a significant role in overall health status; estimates on their contribution to health range from 20 to 40 percent.[4] Economic well-being is an essential factor in the mental and physical health of communities, and is considered one of the social determinants of health (SDOH). A report released by the Robert Wood Johnson Foundation defines SDOH as, "...nonmedical factors such as employment, income, housing, transportation, child care, education, discrimination, and the quality of the places where people live, work, learn, and play,

[1] United Health Foundation, "America's Health Rankings, Comparison with Other Nations, 2016 Annual Report," 2016, available at https://www.americashealthrankings.org/learn/reports/2016-annual-report/comparison-with-other-nations

[2] Bridget C. Booske, Jessica K. Athens, David A. Kindig, Hyojun Park and Patrick L. Remington, "Different perspectives for assigning weights to determinants of health," University of Wisconsin: Population Health Institute, February 2010, available at http://www.countyhealthrankings.org/sites/default/files/differentPerspectivesForAssigningWeights ToDeterminantsOfHealth.pdf

[3] Lenny Bernstein, "U.S. life expectancy declines for the first time since 1993," The Washington Post, December 8, 2016, available at https://www.washingtonpost.com/national/health-science/us-life-expectancy-declines-for-the-first-time-since-1993/2016/12/07/7dcdc7b4-bc93-11e6-91ee-1adddfe36cbe_story.html

[4] Bridget C. Booske, Jessica K. Athens, David A. Kindig, Hyojun Park and Patrick L. Remington, "Different perspectives for assigning weights to determinants of health," University of Wisconsin: Population Health Institute, February 2010, available at http://www.countyhealthrankings.org/sites/default/files/differentPerspectivesForAssigningWeights ToDeterminantsOfHealth.pdf

which influence health. They are 'social' in the sense that they are shaped by social policies."[5] Financial stability not only provides access to many of the resources necessary for a healthy life, but is also necessary to positively respond to life's many challenges. This resilience, or the ability to "bounce back" from adverse situations, can be diminished by financial insecurity at the individual, family and community levels. The consequences of this distress are costly, and are felt far beyond neighborhoods, census tracts and zip codes.

COMMUNITY FINANCIAL HEALTH

There are many opportunities for collaboration among stakeholders that influence the social determinants of health. Economic development within communities remains a challenging SDOH to address within disadvantaged communities, but resources can be aligned to meet complex financial and health needs in ways that advance equity. Anchor institutions, institutions that are rooted in communities and have strong ties to residents through investments, employment and the provision of services, play an important role in the overall well-being of individuals within their service areas. Because of this, the ways in which anchor institutions engage or exclude community members from decisions has a profound effect on overall health. Historical injustices such as redlining and discriminatory lending practices inflicted further disadvantage upon certain communities, and created vulnerability among previously vibrant communities. The impact of these actions reverberates today and is manifested through high unemployment rates, low economic activity and poor infrastructure within neighborhoods targeted by these practices. When a vital component of well-being like economic stability is weakened, individual and community health deteriorates as well.

---

[5] P. Braverman, E. Arkin, T. Orleans, D. Proctor and A. Plough, "What is Health Equity? And What Difference Does a Definition Make?" Robert Wood Johnson Foundation, May 2017, available at https://www.rwjf.org/en/library/research/2017/05/what-is-health-equity-.html

PUBLIC POLICY

As practitioners in the financial and public health fields work to develop responses to these injustices, it is important to recognize that their actions can either create or perpetuate existing inequities, or prevent and reduce them. Activities designed to remedy historical injustices will not fully realize their positive impact unless those affected by these policies are fully engaged as partners in the planning, development, implementation, evaluation, dissemination and allocation of resources designated for these initiatives. There must be a conscious effort to recognize the strengths and assets of communities, and prevent inflicting further disadvantage upon marginalized and vulnerable populations. Leading these efforts with equity will not only eliminate longstanding barriers, but will also raise the bar for everyone.

CRA AS A TOOL FOR THRIVING COMMUNITIES

The Community Reinvestment Act serves as a resource to combat economic inequities, and consequently improve community health. The activities, projects and initiatives that have been implemented through the CRA improve the stability of communities – but the potential is much greater. Financial institutions can play a significant role in promoting the health of the most disadvantaged residents in their service areas. Investing in health amplifies social and economic dividends through larger and stronger workforces, reduced financial burdens on the healthcare sector, reductions in "brain drain" from underinvested neighborhoods and even the opportunity for overlooked talent and intellect to be recognized and used to restore community resilience. CRA practitioners should seek to fund activities and projects that align with other strategic health plans that incorporate the social determinants of health. Community members most impacted by historical injustices and disadvantage should be actively engaged as partners in CRA community development activities and not solely viewed as recipients of services. Opportunities for public health and financial professionals to collaborate on health-promoting activities should also be explored and maximized. Although there are various frameworks within each field to conceptualize economic development and implement positive solutions, the potential for collective impact is significant and should not be ignored.

Health is influenced by and influences most aspects of lived experience. Ensuring that investments are made to address economic security as a social determinant of health will result in thriving communities where everyone can enjoy the benefits of a shared culture of health.

ARIEL ARTHUR is a passionate, engaged public health professional with a focus on issues of equity and justice. She graduated from The George Washington University in May 2014 with a B.A. in Biological Sciences and a minor in Public Health. Ariel currently works as a Health Policy Analyst with the Kentucky Department for Public Health's Office of Health Equity to reduce inequities throughout the commonwealth. Her work in the Chronic Disease Prevention Branch includes addressing issues of asthma and colon cancer. Ariel is a California native and has also lived in Atlanta and Washington D.C. Now that she calls Kentucky home, she enjoys working to ensure all populations she serves achieve the highest level of well-being.

THE HIDDEN NEED: SERVING LOW-INCOME INDIVIDUALS IN AFFLUENT COMMUNITIES

Carrie Gerard
Eastern Area Community Ministries

The American dream is alive in suburbia.

But for low-income families, the opportunity to achieve this dream may only exist if one can access crucial assistance with the necessary supports. And that isn't so easy. Every day, lower-income Americans fight to hold their ground in the desirable neighborhoods of affluent communities despite the challenges they face. Stability, even within these pricier communities, can be achieved, but not without strategic partnerships, particularly relationships with not-for-profit providers, government agencies and progressive private initiatives interested in promoting family stability and security.

Eastern Area Community Ministries (EACM) is one such strategic partner for families striving for stability within an affluent area. EACM provides emergency and supportive services to families in seven zip codes in the northeast quadrant of Jefferson County, Kentucky. The top three wealthiest zip codes within Jefferson County are located within EACM's service area.[1] Well-kept neighborhoods adjacent to well-maintained schools with attractive playground equipment within minutes of moderate to luxury shopping are plentiful. Within this geographic area of the city, not one, but two large YMCA facilities exist as well as the E.P. "Tom" Sawyer State Park. No one could be questioned for choosing to find residence within this area for the amenities it provides.

But how does a family that seeks the same amenities and advantages of this middle- to upper-income geographic area meet the economic responsibilities of residency with only one, or possibly two, jobs that pay just slightly better than minimum wage? The National Low-Income Housing Coalition's report, "Out of Reach, 2017," reveals an equation that just doesn't add up for lower-income families seeking to locate in upper-income communities.

This report says that the average rent in the Louisville market for a two-bedroom apartment is $793.[2] This number is actually low for the seven zip codes of EACM's area. Even a cursory review of two-bedroom rental costs in northeast Jefferson County will yield no results under $1,000. In order to afford housing at this more

---

[1] Allison Stines, "Louisville's Wealthiest ZIP Codes," Louisville Business First, July 20, 2017, available at https://www.bizjournals.com/louisville/subscriber-only/2017/07/14/louisvilles-wealthiest-zip-codes.html

[2] National Low Income Housing Coalition, "Out of Reach 2017: Kentucky," available at http://nlihc.org/oor/kentucky

accurate level, the head of household must be minimally employed at a full-time pay rate of at least $19/hour, or $40,000 annually, while the average renter's wage is only $11.46. That is $10,000 higher than the annual household income of the 18,000 residents identified by the 2010 census as living at or below 200 percent of the Federal Poverty Line within EACM's zip code area. For families attempting to maintain security within these zip codes, it is imperative that they reach out to a partner to strategize increasing their household income.

Employment within this pay scale does exist in this geographic area. But one thing is for sure – a reliable automobile is a *must*. While public transit exists in Metro Louisville, including bus service within suburban corridors, it is meant primarily as a means for higher-skilled workers to access express routes to the downtown business district for first-shift employment.

In fact, these more-affluent neighborhoods are designed for maximum safety and curb appeal, so bus stops are not located within them, but rather along major arteries adjacent to the neighborhoods. This often requires a park-and-ride experience, meaning that in order to access public transportation, a car is necessary to travel to the bus stop. Adding to that difficulty, these routes are not available on weekends or holidays.

In a community meeting held by EACM in July 2016, participants voiced their concern over this issue, asserting that while plenty of East/West routes (suburbs to downtown) exist in Louisville, there are no direct North/South routes to take employees to the Bluegrass Industrial Park from the northeastern suburbs. The routes and schedules published online by Louisville's bus service, TARC, corroborate this fact as a legitimate concern.[3]

---

[3] TARC.com, "Routes & Schedules," available at https://www.ridetarc.org/maps-schedule

Car ownership relieves challenging mobility obstacles, but with it comes the added expenses of maintenance, fuel and insurance. Aside from this added economic responsibility for a household, recognizing the absolute necessity of having an automobile again means linking to a knowledgeable community partner – in this case, one that can connect individuals with programs that lead to reliable transportation (Goodwill's Cars to Work Program, for example).

After providing support for basic needs in the form of a food pantry and emergency financial assistance for utilities and housing costs for over 40 years, EACM began to question what other programming was needed to really stabilize families in our neighborhoods. Disbursing food and paying utility bills was applying "band aids" to our families' gaping wounds. The services were not adequately addressing the unique needs of families seeking to find economic stability within a more affluent setting.

And thus, Pathway to Possibilities at EACM was conceived. It provides individualized case management and goal setting services to help families reach economic stability. Coupled with our traditional services to meet acute needs, such as food insecurity and utility cut-off notices, our families are now experiencing success in gaining longer-term stability.

For example, Susan, a single mother of two children, was tired of continually juggling act her finances and budget. Each month felt like a puzzle to manipulate payment schedules, manage late fees and utilize borrowing tactics. Before discovering EACM's Pathways to Possibilities, Susan's use of supportive services was virtually nil in eastern Jefferson County for two key reasons: (1) availability and accessibility; and (2) awareness of the resources that were available. The closest food stamp office is over 15 miles away from her home; employment services are located at an even greater distance; and child care options, while plentiful, fell well outside her price point, as their businesses were targeted to higher income clientele. Her financial life was spiraling out of control, and she was at risk of losing her job and her home. Since she lives in a neighborhood where accessing social services is not common practice, she wasn't aware of available services nearby and other services were inaccessible due to distance and schedule constraints.

Fortunately, Susan eventually found Pathways to Possibilities at EACM while obtaining assistance with a delinquent utility bill. Success and stability for Susan came once she was able to access an array of coordinated support services designed to address her particular situation. She first sat down with a Family Advocate who helped her define a path to success and set goals. She also met with a volunteer financial education counselor who helped prioritize her expenses and maximize her budget. But attitude changes and improved organization alone were not enough. For three months, the Pathways to Possibilities program invested financial assistance for housing, child care and additional job training to increase her employability factors.

In all, EACM invested approximately $3,500 into helping Susan's situation. The breathing room created by this supportive financial investment gave Susan the space to make the necessary changes that would empower her to lead a financially viable and secure life. And on the other side, Susan had gained sound financial decision-making skills and increased household income from a new job with higher pay, as well as connecting to child care assistance that offset her monthly costs.

EACM has been engaged in family stability programming consistently for three years. The biggest takeaway for us and for our families is that short-term, individualized financial supports must be in place for success to happen. EACM's experience with families challenged in making ends meet in affluent areas, families like Susan's, is that the support systems are limited – both in number and resources provided. And even when present, traditional support for basic needs like food and utility assistance is not enough to bridge the gap from drowning in despair to successful and thrivent living.

This individualized financial support takes funding – and lots of it. The Pathways to Possibilities program is only viable with support from community partners such as local banks and other private businesses. While EACM receives municipal funding for its emergency assistance funding, EACM relies 100 percent on private contributions for Family Stability services.

This progressive investment from private sources can make a huge impact in our community. Crucial investment in families seeking stability allows the process to work. And it does work. More stories like Susan's are possible with sustained community funding for programs like Pathways to Possibilities that invest in people. With continued viability through contributions from private sources, EACM will see the day where its vision is fulfilled of a community where every person is empowered to be fed, sheltered and safe.

CARRIE GERARD is the Executive Director of Eastern Area Community Ministries, a role she has held since 2008. She earned her Bachelors of Arts in Religious Studies from the College of Wooster and holds a Master in Divinity in Theology from Yale Divinity School. Carrie lives in Louisville, Kentucky with her husband, Brian, and sons Ethan and Graham.

BUILD A FINANCIAL EDUCATION CULTURE AT YOUR BANK

Gary Roan
Old National Bank

If there is one rule I've learned in my 30 years as a banker, it's this: A bank can only be as strong as the communities it serves. When we do our part to lift up the most at-risk individuals and families within these communities – through a variety of tools, strategies and resources – our cities and towns become stronger, as do our organizations. As Community Development Banking Manager for Old National Bank, I'm proud that we have implemented a comprehensive approach to community development, including a strong emphasis on financial education.

FINANCIAL EDUCATION AS A CORE ORGANIZATIONAL FOCUS

To some extent, Old National has made financial education a core organizational focus because it's simply the right thing to do, and because doing so is consistent with our values. Yet our commitment to financial education also represents a dollars and cents calculation of the tremendous cost of financial *illiteracy* to our communities.

Consider the following statistics...

- In March of this year, the National Financial Educators Council[1] asked a cross-section of Americans a question: *Across your entire lifetime, about how much money do you think you have lost because you lacked knowledge about personal finances?* A full 33 percent of respondents reported lifetime losses over $15,000, and another 25 percent said they've lost over $30,000 due to a lack of financial knowledge!

- A 2015 Study by the FINRA Foundation[2] (an organization that regulates brokers and Wall Street) found that nearly two-thirds of Americans couldn't pass a basic financial literacy test, while less than half are able to answer basic questions about financial risk!

By addressing this problem head-on, and making financial education an integral part of our approach to community development, Old National is empowering individuals to become

---

[1] National Financial Educators Council, "Financial Illiteracy Costs: Over 3,000 People Estimate How Much," March 2017, available at https://www.financialeducatorscouncil.org/financial-illiteracy-costs/

[2] FINRA Investor Education Foundation, "National Financial Capability Study," 2015, available at https://www.finrafoundation.org/programs/capability/index.html

successful money managers and budgeters, first-time homeowners and, in some cases, even business owners.

How committed is Old National to this process? So much so that we added a Financial Empowerment Director to our Community Development team in 2013, along with a second financial education focused associate in 2016. Additionally, Old National has over 60 associate volunteer financial trainers that continue to raise the bar on Old National's commitment to financial education.

A tremendous example of our unique and powerful approach to financial education is our *12 Steps to Financial Success* program, which earned Old National two American Bankers Association Community Commitment Awards in 2015. Born out of partnership between our Community Development team and the Henderson, Kentucky Detention Center, this first-of-its-kind program was designed to help incarcerated female inmates in Western Kentucky re-enter society as more qualified and financially responsible citizens. In the three years since its inception, we've expanded *12 Steps* into Indiana and Michigan, and it now includes courses geared toward the financial education needs of homeless veterans. Individuals who complete the program are far better equipped to open a bank account, save for college, create an emergency fund, start a business or purchase a home. Topics covered in these one- to two-hour classes include financial psychology, account management, budgeting, credit, ID theft, jobs and careers, entrepreneurship, taxes, investment and retirement.

For many of the incarcerated individuals who complete *12 Steps*, the program represents the first time they have graduated from *any* class or program in their lives, giving them tremendous self-confidence and the motivation they need to break the cycle of financial dependence and poor decision-making that may have contributed to their previous incarceration. For homeless veterans who complete the program, *12 Steps* provides the money management and budgeting skills they desperately need to better position themselves to become homeowners or home renters in the future.

A COMMITMENT TO COLLABORATION

Another critical part of the equation is the fact that our Community Development team partners very closely with the Old National Bank Foundation, which is committed to allocating 80 percent of its grant funds to CRA-eligible initiatives. Our Foundation and Community Development teams have been under the same Community & Social Responsibility Department umbrella since 2011, and members of the two teams share a common office environment, making it easy to share ideas and discuss goals.

Prior to 2011, Old National's Community Development team (which at that time did not focus heavily on financial education) was part of the bank's Compliance department and therefore lacked the close connection we now enjoy with the Foundation team. Today, Community Development and our Foundation work so closely together that it's inconsequential how a particular relationship gets started. What matters is that we collaborate to provide each business partner with multiple resources, including robust financial education resources.

A perfect illustration of this collaboration at work can be found in Old National's partnership with the Community Action Program of Evansville and Vanderburgh County (CAPE). Not only did CAPE receive Old National Bank Foundation funds to build three CRA-eligible rental homes in rural Oakland City, Indiana, our Community Development team also worked with CAPE to provide desperately needed financial education resources.

There are many other examples like this one, each of which helps to paint an overall picture of Community Development and Foundation synergy. Yet it's important to note that we did not arrive here overnight, and that we continue to search daily for better ways to work together for the benefit of our communities.

IT ALL COMES DOWN TO STRENGTHENING LIVES

While financial education is an incredibly strong focus at Old National, it's just one tool in our Community Development toolbox. We're equally committed to community investment, community lending and community outreach & service.

The end goal of all these efforts is simple: to strengthen lives and help create a brighter future for the most at-risk members of our communities. We believe our unique, aggressive approach to financial education is helping us achieve this critical goal.

GARY ROAN is a native of Columbus, Ohio and joined Old National Bank in 2012 to direct the bank's Community Development department. In his five years at the helm, Old National's Community Development team has earned multiple awards related to financial education as well as an Outstanding CRA Rating form the OCC. Gary began his career in banking in 1979 as a lender for Ohio National Bank in Columbus and has held multiple banking and lending positions in his esteemed career.

CHOICES MATTER: CREATING EDUCATION OPTIONS FOR LOW-INCOME STUDENTS

Kerri Vaughan
AAA Scholarship Foundation

Imagine not having the opportunity for your child to attend the school that you want, and in some cases, need for them to attend, whether it is to support your child's current needs or to position them for success later in life. Before 2001, across our nation, most economically-disadvantaged students had no viable alternative to their zoned public schools. That was until three words: "Parental School Choice."

A BRIEF HISTORY OF STATE TAX CREDIT SCHOLARSHIPS

Parental school choice allows education funding to follow students to the schools that best meet their learning needs despite their zone of residency. In 2001, Florida and Pennsylvania enacted the first corporate tax credit scholarship programs, creating a unique opportunity for companies to partner with nonprofit organizations and families in an effort to create expanded educational opportunities for economically-disadvantaged K-12 school-children.

State corporate tax credit scholarship programs allow companies who pay corporate and other types of taxes to receive a tax credit if they redirect their state tax liability to a state-approved 501(c)(3) nonprofit scholarship granting organization (SGO), such as the AAA Scholarship Foundation. The SGO then uses these redirected tax dollars to fund scholarships for low-income, disabled and/or displaced-children to attend the school (up to grade 12) that best meets their unique learning needs.

Because the first two programs in Florida and Pennsylvania proved so effective, as of 2017, there are now corporate tax credit scholarship programs in 17 states. Of course, each corporate tax credit scholarship program varies from state to state. Some states offer a dollar-for-dollar tax credit (Alabama, Arizona, Florida, Georgia and Nevada) to participating corporations, while others offer between 50 to 90 percent tax credit for the corporation's tax redirection. Additionally, while most of the programs limit scholarship eligibility based on certain income levels or other attributes of the applicants or families, many do not. States that do limit student participation by income include Arizona, Alabama, Florida and Nevada.

The majority of these programs also place requirements and restrictions on the SGOs. Most common are requirements that a certain portion of donations must be used for scholarships, which usually allow for a modest portion to cover administrative costs. Other typical scholarship organization requirements relate to data reporting, how scholarship decisions are made, certification, employee background checks, student testing and financial auditing. Because a corporation's tax redirection is such a gift to the children it serves, it is crucial that the corporation chooses the right SGO to be a good steward of their funds. Due diligence is advised before participating in any state corporate tax credit scholarship program.

THE AAA SCHOLARSHIP FOUNDATION APPROACH

Currently, the AAA Scholarship Foundation is the only state approved scholarship organization in the United States that is approved to manage state corporate tax credit scholarship programs in six states exclusively serving low-income and/or disabled or displaced children.

At AAA Scholarship Foundation, we only participate in state programs that offer a high-yield tax credit opportunity for donors: Alabama, Arizona, Florida, Georgia and Nevada, which provide corporate donors with a dollar-for-dollar tax credit; and Pennsylvania, which provides up to a 90 percent tax credit. We only award scholarships to low-income, disabled and/or displaced children, even if the state program allows for higher-income scholarship recipients or does not have income restrictions, such as in Georgia. We are committed to ensuring that our AAA scholarships are awarded to those students in greatest financial need.

AAA provides companies with the convenience and efficiency of a single solution for participating in multiple state tax credit scholarship programs, enabling companies to meet their tax and philanthropic goals in one or more states. There are many other aspects that set the AAA Scholarship Foundation apart from other SGOs. For example, the AAA Scholarship Foundation:

- Has been awarded the prestigious GuideStar Platinum Seal, demonstrating the highest level of transparency practices in a nonprofit organization;
- Awards scholarships directly to families – not schools;
- Awards scholarships solely to qualifying low-income, disabled and/or displaced students;
- Awards scholarships for at least a 3-year term in states that allow multi-year commitments – we believe that the continuity of an educational setting is important for children to succeed;
- Is managed by the nation's leading state corporate tax credit scholarship program professionals with over 15 years of experience successfully administering programs;
- Has a CPA on staff to ensure that company's tax questions are answered correctly and to ensure timely and accurate reporting; and
- Limits overhead costs to 4.14 percent for administrative funding (3 percent in Florida).

WHY PARENTAL SCHOOL CHOICE MATTERS

Since 2001, state corporate tax credit scholarship programs have proven to be a beneficial opportunity for corporations, families and communities as a whole. The programs are extremely popular with the families they serve, as well as the companies that participate, because they give at-risk students an increased chance at a brighter future and give companies the satisfaction that they are utilizing their tax dollars toward building a better educated workforce.

Many children who participate in these programs are either performing at below grade level, failing at their previous school or both when they receive a corporate tax credit scholarship. Parents who find their children in these circumstances and care about their future look for viable options. They seek an atmosphere that challenges their child and will reverse inadequate learning, social patterns and the potential lifelong negative impact. They wish to change their child's learning environment, acquaintances and the unfortunate, predictable outcomes associated with school failure. For low-income children, who are often several grade levels behind their peers, these programs are a lifeline for paving a pathway out of poverty. By simply redirecting their taxes, companies make a life-changing difference for a child.

Initially, states implemented state corporate tax credit scholarship programs as a tool to increase overall graduation rates in areas of high poverty. Poverty has been shown to play a key role in lowering graduation rates. Early proponents of tax credit scholarship programs sought to provide additional educational opportunities for low-income children in an effort to change that dynamic, but they found that this was just one of the benefits. The wider impact that these programs provide is why they have been duplicated in multiple states.

Studies have found that the state corporate tax credit scholarship programs:

- Incur significant tax savings for states where they are implemented. Typically, the scholarship awarded to the student to attend a school of their choice is significantly lower than the cost to educate the same child in their district assigned school. In 2014, a study showed that Pennsylvania saved closed to $800 million through its tax credit scholarship program annually[1], and in Florida, the

---

[1] Andrew LeFevre, "Ten Thousand Lifeboats: Improving Students' Educational Features via Pennsylvania's Scholarship Tax Credit Programs," Policy Brief from the Commonwealth Foundation, Vol 26, No. 1, September 2014 available at

Office of Program Policy Analysis Government Accountability found that the tax credit scholarship program saved taxpayers $1.49 for every dollar redirected[2];

- Lower crime rates. A 2016 working paper by DeAgelis and Wolf concluded that parental school choice reduces the proclivity of students to commit crimes[3]; and
- Increase the performance of all schools. In 2010, a report written by Northwestern University economics and social policy professor David Figlio found that the creation of the Florida Tax Credit Scholarship Program led immediately to academic improvement in the public schools as well.[4]

Anecdotally, we have found in our 15+ years of managing these programs that they:

- Empower not just the student who receives the scholarship, but the entire family. We have heard so many stories of parents who go back and get their GED or college diploma. Many scholarship recipients are the first in their family to go on to college, inspiring siblings who do the same;
- Provide a well-trained workforce for the economy. We are able to work with companies to ascertain what skills they

---

http://www.commonwealthfoundation.org/docLib/20140912_PBEITCFinal.pdf

[2] Florida Legislature Office of Program Policy and Analysis and Government Accountability, "Florida Tax Credit Scholarship Program Fiscal Year 2008-09 Fiscal Impact," Research Memorandum, March 1, 2010, available at http://www.fldoe.org/core/fileparse.php/5423/urlt/OPPAGA_March_2010_Report.pdf

[3] Corey A. DeAngelis and Patrick J. Wolf, "The School Choice Voucher: A 'Get Out of Jail' Card?" SSRN.com, March 8, 2016, available at http://papers.ssrn.com/sol3/papers.cfm?abstract_id=2743541

[4] David N. Figlio and Cassandra M.D. Hart, "Competitive Effects of Means-Tested School Vouchers," National Bureau of Economic Research Working Paper No. 16056, June 2010, available at http://www.nber.org/papers/w16056

need and then share this information with our students so they can start to acquire the necessary skills; and

- Build successful public-private partnerships. Because of the direct engagement of businesses in the educational process, where businesses fund scholarships in exchange for state tax credits, these programs are tremendously successful public-private partnerships, oftentimes helping families directly in the communities where the donor companies operate their businesses. Employees are proud to be a part of these programs, realizing that the work that they do often leads to providing a scholarship to a child in their community.

STATE TAX CREDIT SCHOLARSHIP PROGRAMS AS CRA INVESTMENTS

In addition to having a say in where their tax dollars are spent, corporations including banks also enjoy the advantage of an increase in their philanthropic budget without an increase in spending. For financial institutions, there is an added benefit to participating in the state corporate tax credit scholarship program, as examiners at the bank regulatory agencies have approved dollars transferred to fund scholarships through these programs to qualify for positive consideration under the CRA investment test.

Before participating with any SGO, financial institutions need to clarify that the SGO only serves low-income children and compare the scholarship family's income to the median income to determine whether it's at or below 30 percent (extremely low), 50 percent (low) or 80 percent (moderate) of the Area Median Income. The AAA Scholarship Foundation's typical scholarship student is an ethnic minority living with a struggling single parent/caregiver in a high-crime community. More than 85 percent of AAA scholarships are distributed to children at or below 185 percent of poverty.

Although these state corporate state scholarship programs have made significant progress since their inception, a great need still remains. According to the 2016 Annual Grad Report by Civic Enterprises and Everyone Graduates Center at the School of Education at Johns Hopkins University, only 74.6 percent of all low-income students graduated compared to 89 percent of non-low-income students. However, through innovated education initiatives like corporate tax credit scholarship programs, those numbers are getting closer and closer to being equalized.

As we look at the CRA on its milestone 40th anniversary, we are excited to be making a major impact in the lives of low-income students throughout the country. Knowing that banks can empower the immediate and future success of so many students, while still meeting their CRA obligations, is rewarding for everyone involved.

KERRI VAUGHAN has been working in the fundraising arena for more than 20 years. She currently serves as Managing Director for the AAA Scholarship Foundation. AAA is a 501(c)(3) nonprofit organization and approved Scholarship Organization exclusively serving low-income children through Scholarship Tax Credit Programs in six states – Alabama, Arizona, Florida, Georgia, Nevada and Pennsylvania. An exceptional leader, who builds, manages and inspires high-performing teams, she formerly oversaw the development efforts of Step Up For Students and raised more than $1 billion in state tax credit and philanthropic contributions to fuel tax credit scholarship programs in Florida. She is recognized nationally for her fundraising expertise and success, and served on the boards of the Miami-Dade Industrial Development Authority and Consumer Debt Counselors.

A PATH TO EDUCATION FOR HOMELESS AND FOSTER YOUTH

Israel Diaz, Lauren Fernandez and Lorinda Gonzalez
Educate Tomorrow & Grants Ink

Educate Tomorrow is a 501(c)(3) nonprofit organization that provides a path to independence for at-risk homeless and foster youth and similarly disadvantaged young people through specific programs directed towards education, mentoring and life-skills training. It is a sad truth in our country that youth who grow up in foster care or experience homelessness seldom end up with high school diplomas, agency, independence or peace of mind. It is far more likely that violence, early parenthood, addiction, prison bars and fear characterize their futures.

THE PATH BEGINS

In 2003, the Emmons sisters, transplants to the Miami area, through a commitment to social justice, stumbled upon a piece of barely-known Florida legislation. In 1997, Florida Statute 1009.25 set forth that any Floridian who grew up in foster care, was experiencing homelessness or was adopted out of the foster care system, had the opportunity to attend any state college, university or vocational program tuition free. Yet in 2002, nearly every key stakeholder from schools to foster parents, case managers, local leaders and of course, the youth themselves, were unaware of this opportunity and not actively promoting it. The Florida University System reported that in the 2002-2003 academic year, just eight students utilized the tuition and fee waiver at a university in Florida despite thousands being eligible.

In an effort to end this cycle of delinquency, poverty and dependence, the Emmons sisters quickly founded Educate Tomorrow with an ethos of Independence Through Education. Education is proven to be a leading indicator of adult success and Dr. Ruby K. Payne, author of "A Framework for Understanding Poverty," states that the most prominent reason of the four reasons people leave poverty is "someone 'sponsors' them." Knowing this, the sisters decided that every young person who has experienced abandonment, homelessness or abuse should have an educational mentor to help them realize their potential, and that this support should be a constant.

SUPPORTING THOSE IN NEED

Studies have shown that foster youth are often overlooked and unprepared for adulthood. Instability, trauma, neglect and abuse set up foster youth to be more likely to fail than succeed. According to a 2014 study on the educational outcomes of children in foster care, only 20 percent of foster youth who graduate from high school will attend college and less than 5 percent will end up graduating from college. Less than 60 percent of foster youth in Florida will complete high school and 75 percent are behind one grade level while attending school.

There are a multitude of noble and impactful charities that help vulnerable youth in incredible ways, but almost all these services conclude for young people after their 18th birthday or high school graduation, leaving them with the rug figuratively pulled out from under them. Educate Tomorrow is unique in our belief that we are a family to all our students who never had a nurturing family environment. You never "age out" of a family, and Educate Tomorrow believes in creating a continuum of care by staying engaged with our youth through graduation, college, graduate school, employment and beyond. We know that 92 percent of our students have a high school diploma or the equivalent by age 20; and 42 percent of our students over age 25 have a post-secondary degree or certificate, which is better than the general population in the United States and much better than the estimated 1 percent to 3 percent of former foster youth in Florida and nationally. Less than 1 percent of our students have problems with the law and less than 10 percent are experiencing issues with homelessness. Studies have drawn a direct link between academic success and being linked to a support system that cares.

Reflecting on our recent momentum, Educate Tomorrow has increased services, multiplied our number of college graduates tenfold and grown our budget 330 percent in the past five years. Students join our family at any point in their teenage or young adult years and may begin to receive services, as well as get paired with a mentor, as early as 13 years old. The Children's Trust of Miami-Dade County has funded Educate Tomorrow for the past 10 years, and recently increased their funding from $100,000 to $405,000 in 2016. In 2017, it awarded Educate Tomorrow $3.1 million over the next four years to be the leading agency in Miami-

Dade County supporting foster and at-risk youth. The Children's Trust reports that over a twelve-month period, "Educate Tomorrow's mentees show increases in their school enrollment, life skills knowledge and general self-efficacy."

THE EDUCATE TOMORROW DIFFERENCE

Our vision is to ultimately provide a continuum of care for all youth who have been subjected to poverty, abuse, abandonment and/or neglect by striving to make higher education an attainable goal. Our programs are primarily designed to help youth and young adults by providing them with multi-year, goal-oriented academic and career coaching, intensive skill-building and life enrichment activities and workshops.

Educate Tomorrow fills in the gaps for foster youth and creates a supportive community where no one ever "ages out." Thanks to Educate Tomorrow, vulnerable foster youth now have allies alongside them for life to help them succeed in their continuing path into adulthood. By partnering with local colleges and universities, Educate Tomorrow provides mentoring, social support and life skills coaching to "aged-out" foster youth.

Working in partnership with Florida International University and Miami Dade College, Educate Tomorrow has designed programs that have proven successful in affecting "aged out" individuals in a positive and life-altering way. As a result of the impact and success of this program, over time Educate Tomorrow has had to open a "Drop-In Center" at their local office. This facility, which is centrally located in Miami-Dade County, provides a social support system in which our target population can find a steady and trusted place for academic tutoring and other key resources.

Students enrolled in Educate Tomorrow's mentoring, life skills and education programs have proven to be more successful than foster youth who are not. For example, over 90 percent of our students have earned a high school diploma or GED equivalent and over 40 percent have been able to complete a post-secondary degree or certificate. Life Coaches and Educational Mentoring Specialists, who are trained specifically to deal with our target population, are committed to setting them up for success by educating them to navigate a variety of systems to ensure continued positive growth towards their specific goals. Lifelong success is attained by identifying individual specific goals and measuring outcomes based on progress towards those goals. Over the past two years, Educate Tomorrow has celebrated 52 college graduates including seven Master's degrees, one Juris Doctorate and one Dental Doctorate. All of these students were able to attend college tuition-free using Florida's DCF or Homeless waiver. We are working in partnership with the foster care system in Miami-Dade County, with Miami-Dade County Public Schools, Miami Dade College and Florida International University, as well as dozens of youth development organizations that do quality work in our community. Together we are making a profound impact on the lives of these youth and young adults.

As others in Educate Tomorrow's network have watched the inspiring and life-changing work being done, there have been invitations to replicate our model in other cities across the country. Educate Tomorrow is currently working on national expansion in San Antonio, Texas, Ft. Collins, Colorado and San Francisco, California, as well as regional growth in South Florida into Palm Beach County.

CRA'S ROLE IN EDUCATE TOMORROW

We know that the Community Reinvestment Act was initially created to support communities in obtaining access to credit. However, over the past 40 years, CRA has been updated to include consideration of community development investments and services that banks provide or support. Much like CRA's target population, our youth and young adults are struggling with basic needs including shelter, life skills and the ability to become self-sufficient. As CRA supports banks' efforts in meeting the basic needs of their communities, in turn, banks can and have supported Educate Tomorrow in meeting the same needs for our youth and young adults.

We know, as do bankers, that the need is great and seems endless. That is why we strive every day to provide real support and education advancement opportunities for our target population. As we look to the future, both locally in South Florida and through our national expansion, we know that banks and their CRA efforts will continue to be a key supporter of our growth and ultimately our youth and young adults. Together, we can provide the education that the country needs to ensure success in all of our communities.

ISRAEL DIAZ is the Senior Business Development for Grants Ink, an organization that has provided support to Educate Tomorrow in its growth and expansion. He has over 10 years experience in the fundamentals of organizing and restructuring nonprofit organizations. He has assisted multiple businesses in establishing policies and procedures to help their daily operations run smoothly. Israel has a Bachelor's Degree in Public Administration and managed grants for 10 years at Miami Dade College.

LAUREN FERNANDEZ is the Project Liaison for Grants Ink and holds a Bachelor's of Arts Degree in Interdisciplinary Social Studies from the University of South Florida. With a decade of experience in nonprofits, she is familiar with the nature of grants and the crucial role they plan in program expansion. Lauren is inspired by the work her clients do for the community and is honored to partner with organizations that bring more goodness to the world.

LORINDA GONZALEZ is a graduate of Florida Atlantic University where she earned a Bachelor's of Arts Degree in English Writing and Rhetoric. She is currently completing graduate work towards her Master's Degree in Mass Communication and Marketing at Southern New Hampshire University. Lorinda has a passion for training fellow grant writers and sharing insider tips and tricks with nonprofit organizations for acquiring grant funds, which she has shared in over 100 workshops. She brings more than 10 years experience to the Grants Ink team leading to over $8 million in awarded grant funding.

DIGITAL INCLUSION: OVERCOMING BARRIERS TO SELF-SUFFICIENCY

Ed Blayney
Louisville Metro Government

Today, participation in society relies on the ability to access and use the Internet effectively. Whether applying for a job at a fast food restaurant, doing homework or starting a business, everyone needs digital skills, tools and connectivity to fully participate in modern society. These factors are increasingly becoming the choke points that prevent thousands of our fellow citizens from adapting to and accessing the benefits of a knowledge-driven, innovative economy.

As more and more of modern life moves online, the gap between the digital haves and have-nots will only continue to widen. These divides mirror racial, socioeconomic and geographic inequities in our community and nation as a whole. The impacts of digital inequities extend into the workplace, into our schools and can significantly impact citizens' abilities to access government services and participate in civic society. Without action, we will continue to limit socio-economic mobility in our community and may hold back whole segments of our society from reaching their highest potential.

To increase opportunities for economic development, educational attainment and civic participation, stronger neighborhoods and local business districts and an enhanced quality of life for all residents, Louisville, Kentucky created a comprehensive plan to promote digital inclusion in our community: digitalinclusion.louisvilleky.gov. Digital Inclusion is a nationally recognized term for the efforts to reduce, and eventually eliminate, the digital divide. In the long term, Louisville's plan aims to increase socioeconomic mobility and job attainment for our residents. In the short term, this plan is a starting point for pilot projects, grant applications and finding new strategic partners to meet these goals.

STRATEGIC FOCUS AREAS

The plan has three key strategic focus areas to address the digital divide in Louisville:

1. Improving Connectivity: To achieve digital inclusion, all citizens must be able to access affordable, convenient, reliable, fast and full (not exclusively mobile) Internet access. The problem is partly infrastructure and partly affordability. Internet access should be available in Louisville in the same way as water or electricity.

2. Teaching Digital Skills: Train residents in digital skills to increase their employability and ability to participate in modern society.

3. Providing Hardware and Technical Support: Louisville citizens need adequate and affordable hardware, assistive technology and technical support for those devices. Gaps exist across racial and socioeconomic lines nationwide in terms of laptop and desktop ownership. To take advantage of job and community opportunities, all residents need reliable access to a computer, not just a smartphone.

Since we first drafted our plan in July 2016 (officially released in May 2017), we have started to take action to address some of our identified socio-economic and racial disparities in Louisville. First and foremost was building a strong coalition of internal partners that are already working on digital inclusion and serving our intended audience. In our discussion with our partners about their initiatives and the needs of the people they work with, we decided that we would focus first on the connectivity and hardware issues for residents.

We started there based on a review of the relevant statistics and the anecdotal evidence from frontline employees directly engaging residents. From this analysis it was clear that we needed to focus on connecting more of our residents to the Internet and getting more computers into people's homes.

Our review of home Internet access found that one's ability to access the Internet and a computer at home depended a lot on household income and race. Nationally, African-American households are 16 percentage points less likely to have an Internet connection at home while Hispanic households and Native American households, respectively, are 11 and 19 percentage points less likely to have an Internet connection at home.[1]

---

[1] Council of Economic Advisers, "Mapping the Digital Divide," July 2015, available at https://obamawhitehouse.archives.gov/sites/default/files/wh_digital_divide_issue_brief.pdf

Locally, our challenges mirror those at the national level, but may be more pronounced. Among the 50 largest metropolitan statistical areas (MSAs) in the United States, Louisville ranks 46th in terms of home Internet connectivity, with a three-year average of just 75.7 percent of residents reporting in-home Internet.[2] Specifically, considering the area over which Louisville Metro Government has jurisdiction, Jefferson County ranks 30th among principal cities of the 50 largest metro areas.[3] Data shows that it is some of the most in-need populations that do not have access to the resources necessary to achieve in our modern economy.

The 2015 American Community Survey provides the following statistics related to Internet adoption and usage in Louisville:

Percentage of households with a home Internet by education-level:
- Less than high school – 41.8 percent
- High school less than college – 72.7 percent
- Bachelors degree or higher – 90.1 percent

Percentage of households with an Internet connection by employment status:
- Employed 81.6 percent
- Unemployed – 64.6 percent

Percentage of households without a home Internet connection:
- White – 8.3 percent
- Black – 24.4 percent
- Asian – 4.6 percent
- Hispanic – 13.6 percent

---

[2] Caroline Toblert and Karen Mossberger, "U.S. Current Population Survey & American Community Survey Geographic Estimates of Internet Use, 1997-2014," Harvard Dataverse, 2015, available at https://dataverse.harvard.edu/dataset.xhtml?persistentId=doi:10.7910/DVN/UKXPZX

[3] Ibid.

Percentage of households with an internet connection by income:
- Less than $20K – 8.6 percent
- $20K to $74K – 29.1 percent
- $75K or more – 8.3 percent

Some have said that smartphones have closed the device gap, but in Louisville, we do not believe that a smartphone by itself provides an adequate digital resource for modern life. Anyone who has ever tried to write an essay, complete an assignment or fill out an application on a small screen will tell you the challenges it poses. To take advantage of job, educational and community opportunities, everyone needs reliable access to a computer (desktop or laptop), not just a smartphone. When we dove into the stats for computer ownership, we found similar disparities. Further, frontline service employees shared that home Internet access and computer ownership may not be mutually exclusive issues for the people they work with every day. Based on their experience with community members, people often forgo home Internet access because they lack a computer (or have an inadequate computer) and vice versa. Access to computers in a home varies by race in Louisville, as well:

Percentage of households without a computer by race:
- White – 10.6 percent
- Black – 17 percent
- Hispanic – 20.9 percent

Percentage of households without a computer by employment status:
- Employed – 7.1 percent
- Unemployed – 12.6 percent
- Out of workforce – 24.2 percent

With these challenges in mind, we started working towards getting more people connected to the Internet at home and getting more computers to those without them. Working with frontline service agencies, we look for opportunities to add digital inclusion work into current initiatives that directly connect with the groups most likely to need to be connected with the Internet and a computer.

The first pilot project we started involved both the Louisville Free Public Library (LFPL) and the Community Services & Resiliency (CSR) Department. We came together around the idea that getting people a reliable connection to the Internet and a computer would help with outcomes for participants in their self-sufficiency program. Through their Tech Soup program, the LFPL was able to procure affordable mobile data hotspots that had a recurring cost of $10 per month for unlimited data. We were also able to secure 15 lightly used Chromebooks from around Metro Government. With both the connectivity and hardware issues solved, we worked with CSR to distribute the items and follow-up with clients monthly, and conduct an interview six months into the pilot. The result of this pilot so far – which still has months to go – has been overwhelmingly positive. It shows that even a small investment when partnered with the right program can have a significant impact on people's lives.

To make an impact on a larger scale, we started a campaign for families to sign up for low-cost Internet plans available through local Internet Service Providers (ISP). In Louisville, two ISPs offer low-cost Internet plans for families receiving government benefits ranging from Supplemental Nutrition Assistance Program (SNAP) benefits to free and reduced lunch. Again, we reached out to partners in our community directly working with those that may be most in-need. We found willing partners in the Louisville Metro Housing Authority (LMHA) and CSR. With the LMHA, we taught the case managers for their largest housing complex, Beecher Terrace, about both of the programs and how they could facilitate signing people up for the plans. Additionally, we started showing up to resident meetings and events to spread the word and help people sign up. We partnered with CSR for back-to-school events throughout the community to help spread the word about these programs and help people sign up for low-cost Internet. In the first six weeks of this program, we were able to sign up over 200 families for the Internet and distribute hundreds of flyers about both programs to interested families.

In tandem with our Internet sign-ups, we started collecting names of families signing up for low-cost Internet that also needed a computer at home, but we needed to tap into reliable sources of computers before we could begin to distribute them. To help find computers, we worked with findCRA to send out a one-page memo asking local banks to donate computers, so that we could get them to people in need. Through their support, we were able to secure good computers in working condition from three local banks through the Community Reinvestment Act. These community partnerships have not only resulted in over 100 computer donations to start our program, but have also allowed us to start developing relationships with these banks, which will hopefully extend many years into the future as we grow and expand the program to serve more people. Right now, we are working with two local high schools to get the computers refurbished and out to the people that we identified during our sign-ups and to in-need high school students. We believe this program will start to provide immediate benefits to both those receiving the computers and the young people refurbishing them. The program is just getting started, but if our success with the low-cost Internet sign-ups is any indication, we are at the start of something special in our community.

As someone who works primarily on technology projects, it is rare to hear that something you work on is a blessing in someone's life, but you regularly hear that when helping people connect to our modern, digital world. The Internet, a reliable computer and the ability to navigate both are requirements to live in the 21st Century.

People without these items realize this fact more than those who take their unfettered access for granted. Unfortunately, technology has created another equity issue that we need to diligently address, if we truly want to have a society that gives everyone a chance to reach his or her fullest potential. By working to close the digital divide through the holistic approach of digital inclusion and programs aligned with CRA, we all can provide immediate and long-term benefits to our communities.

ED BLAYNEY (@edblayney) is an Innovation Project Manager in the Office of Performance Improvement and Innovation (@opi2lou) for Louisville Metro Government (KY) and a 2016 Route 50 Navigator Award recipient. His projects focus on digital inclusion, smart city research and implementation and civic tech. Before joining Louisville Metro, he served as an infantry officer in the U.S. Army and completed his graduate studies at the School of Government at UNC-Chapel Hill.

COMPETITIVE FUNDRAISING: THE GAME WHERE EVERYONE WINS

Reid McDowell
Brackets For Good

More and more organizations across the United States are adopting the practice of concentrated fundraising campaigns and many, such as Girls Who Code, **MENTOR**, Rise Against Hunger and Girl Scouts of the USA are, for the first time, participating in competitive fundraising tournaments, with results to the tune of $3.6M being raised and over 31 percent of donations coming from first-time donors.

Engaging in competitive fundraising efforts with other nonprofits offers many benefits to participating organizations, the most vital of which include increased awareness of a nonprofit's *cause* in donors' minds, better accommodation of donors' needs and preferences and a higher level of donor engagement.

A COMPETITION WHERE EVERYONE WINS

So what is competitive fundraising, and how does it work? Every March, Brackets For Good hosts single-elimination, bracket-style fundraising tournaments across the country that raise much-needed funds and awareness for nonprofit organizations of all sizes. Nonprofits can enter the tournament by December for competition the following March. We select 64 nonprofits for each tournament city; they retain all the donations raised as well as the donor information, regardless of their advancement in the tournament. The tournament takes place in six rounds over five weeks. It truly is a competition where everyone wins – nonprofits, their clients, corporate sponsors and the community as a whole.

Brackets For Good was founded in April 2011, when the entire state of Indiana was bleeding blue and white. While you may be thinking back to what was going on with the Indianapolis Colts in April 2011, we were actually supporting the Butler University men's basketball team. They had made it to their second national championship game in two years. Unfortunately, history couldn't be repeated, as Butler experienced a painful loss. But it was the energy and excitement that was flowing through the city at that time that prompted Brackets For Good's Co-Founders to wonder if the same enthusiasm could be bottled up and put to use for good. That feeling quickly turned into a brainstorm, which lead to the organization's founding.

HOW NONPROFIT COMPETITIVE FUNDRAISING WORKS

Multiple touch points help a nonprofit's cause stick in donors' minds

Big for-profit brands know that it takes many interactions, or brand impressions, with a consumer to alter their behavior or prompt an action. The nonprofit sector – and fundraisers in particular – can learn from these strategies.

For example, auto manufacturers know that a billboard in and of itself isn't enough to make a person buy a car. However, the billboard serves as one touch point among hundreds or thousands of consumer touch points that result in influencing behavior.

In the world of charitable organizations, it's critically important that these touch points aren't strictly pleas for support. To successfully encourage donors to support a nonprofit's cause, these touch points need to communicate impact statistics and stories about beneficiaries, in addition to appeals for financial support.

In a competitive fundraising initiative, support can be solicited through a variety of different communication channels, which gives participating organizations the chance to plan ahead and create multiple touch points with supporters.

It doesn't overburden nonprofit supporters

One of the least talked about – but most essential – skills that charitable fundraising professionals must have is empathy. To hone this skill, fund development and marketing personnel need to put themselves in the shoes of their donors and understand their feelings.

Generally, donors really do care a great deal about the mission of organizations they support, but a nonprofit's cause represents just a small fraction of the things they think and care about in a given week. Competitive fundraising events put a nonprofit's cause on donors' radars in an entertaining way, without overburdening them with too many asks. Additionally, competitive fundraising initiatives generally have predetermined end-dates in mind, so supporters can be invited to participate without worrying about ongoing commitments or open-ended timelines.

To ensure supporters are not overwhelmed, organizations should concentrate fundraising efforts in periodic pulses of activity throughout the year and create new, innovative touch points with supporters to keep them engaged. When a campaign ends, it's important to give them a break before ramping up the next fundraising effort; one of the best ways to lose a supporter is incessantly sending them pleas for support.

Ultimately, competitive fundraising allows a supporter to engage more fully for a short period of time and then, without guilt, lean away to focus time and efforts on other important aspects of their lives.

The element of competition helps donors have fun and feel more engaged

The unique format of a competitive fundraising campaign allows supporters to get involved on a new level and have fun while showing their dedication to a charitable cause.

Donors can share their involvement on social media, create incentives for their friends or coworkers to contribute and, through this enhanced engagement with the cause, find new ways to drive the mission forward.

In recent competitive fundraising tournaments organized by Brackets For Good, 64 percent of the nonprofit supporters reported that their experience rallying behind their favorite organizations made them feel more engaged with the organization they supported. 38 percent reported that they would now be more likely to volunteer with the organization they supported.

A GREATER COLLECTIVE IMPACT FOR COMMUNITIES

Since March 2012 through April 2017, Brackets For Good tournaments have only operated for 32 weeks out of 312 total weeks during that period. During those 32 weeks of tournament operations, we have helped to raise over $6.3 million for local charities in the Ann Arbor area, Baltimore, Cincinnati, Denver, Hartford, Indianapolis, Louisville, Miami, Nashville, St. Louis, the Twin Cities, Washington D.C. and through a National Tournament (featuring 31 different states across the country). In the coming years, we will continue to expand our tournaments. We are proud to share that during that same time period, 31,921 donations were made, with 31.6 percent of those received from first-time donors.

Our tournaments not only support nonprofits in their fundraising efforts, but also offer corporate citizens, including banks, the ability to join in the action. Banks have been key supporters of the local tournaments in many of our cities. In addition, many of the nonprofits that compete in our tournaments conduct CRA-qualified community development activities including affordable housing, job creation, economic empowerment, homeless support, domestic violence advocacy, youth development and other support to low-income communities.

REID MCDOWELL is a cause marketer and social innovator that parlayed for-profit marketing experience into a pursuit to create innovative ways for people to learn about and support charitable nonprofits. Reid co-runs Brackets for Good, focusing much of his time on tournament promotions and strategic partnerships. You can reach Reid at reid@bfg.org. For more information about competitive fundraising tournaments with Brackets for Good, visit www.BFG.org.

EMBRACING CRA TECHNOLOGY

Brian Waters
findCRA

I began my banking career nearly 20 years ago at a local bank as the IRA Administrator. At that time, my IRA Department of one was not on the cutting edge. Over the years, as my career advanced within the bank, so did the bank's technology. First came online banking, and then mobile banking, followed quickly by new advancements each year.

Throughout that time, the Community Reinvestment Act remained an important topic in our growing compliance department. As a group of regulatory analysts, we were continually monitoring, tracking and analyzing our bank's historical performance to pursue an Outstanding examination rating. Every few years, we rushed to compile binders full of information for our examiners. It was the same process on repeat.

A few years ago, I was sitting in a meeting with other bankers and local nonprofit leaders. Thoughts and ideas flowed throughout the room, all about how we could work together to meet our community's needs. I left that room contemplating how the process for relationship building could be better. As the world moved more online, I wondered, why hadn't CRA made the same shift? Why was our process locked in the past?

I began to think about how CRA and technology might work together. Why couldn't we find a way to save time digging through historical reports, spreadsheets and general online searches, and instead develop CRA technology that would proactively support community reinvestment while simultaneously helping our staff make more-informed, quicker decisions? I realized this future was possible, but we would first have to harness three key challenges that have significant impacts on the lives as CRA professionals – the digital shift, data overload and the resource gap.

THE DIGITAL SHIFT

Humanity's growing digital shift is no longer a futurist concept or a hypothetical. Americans have moved nearly all aspects of our lives online. We are living in the world of Star Trek – a technology revolution unseen in the history of the world. Consumers have moved rapidly to digital first interactions, whether in their entertainment, shopping, social connection, dating lives and yes, even banking. A recent KPMG study assessed the U.S. global online shopping market at $1.9 trillion dollars.[1] Netflix streams in

---

[1] KPMG, "The Truth About Online Consumers: 2017 Global Online Consume Report," January 2017, available at https://assets.kpmg.com/content/dam/kpmg/xx/pdf/2017/01/the-truth-about-online-consumers.pdf

over 36 million U.S. homes.[2] Socially, 62 percent of Americans actively use Facebook every month.[3]

Driven by this customer behavior, the nation's banking model and services have also made the digital shift. A recent study by the American Bankers Association looked at the banking needs of millennials, a group that will soon make up 40 percent of the workforce and are the fastest growing customer base for banks.[4] Millennials want to conduct their banking from the palm of their hand, instantly, and wholeheartedly believe that within the next five years, the way we access money will be totally different.[5] Similarly, Baby Boomers, a bank's most loyal and affluent customer base, have also adopted digital banking, with 71 percent using online banking services at least once a week, on par with younger generations.[6]

Nonprofits, some of a bank's key CRA partners, have also adopted technology in pursuit of their mission. A quick online search will identify hundreds of tools that a nonprofit can use in providing its services and a recent study by the Nonprofit Technology Network found that 66 percent of nonprofits surveyed include technology in their strategic plans.[7]

---

[2] Mike Rich, "OTT Breaks Out of Its Netflix Shell," comScore.com, April 10, 2017, available at http://www.comscore.com/Insights/Blog/OTT-Breaks-Out-of-Its-Netflix-Shell

[3] Statista, "Facebook usage penetration in the United States from 2015 to 2022," The Statistics Portal, 2017, available at https://www.statista.com/statistics/183460/share-of-the-us-population-using-facebook/

[4] American Bankers Association, "Millennials and Banking," available at https://www.aba.com/Tools/Infographics/Pages/Infographic-MillennialsBanking.aspx

[5] Ibid.

[6] American Bankers Association, "Banking the Boomers," available at https://www.aba.com/Tools/Infographics/Pages/Infographic-BankingtheBoomers.aspx

[7] Sara Thompson, "Allocating Your Nonprofit's Tech Budget," TechImpact, May 8, 2016, available at http://blog.techimpact.org/allocating-your-nonprofits-tech-budget

Based on this data alone, it appears that everyone, from consumers to banks to nonprofits, has shifted to online and mobile interactions. Why then are we not seeing CRA relationship building moving in that same direction? This leads me to our second challenge – data overload.

DATA OVERLOAD

When I sat down to research interesting facts for this article, I quickly became overloaded with the sheer amount of information available. Every click of the mouse found another study with another notable fact. We each experience this data overload daily.

The most immediate inundation of data that bankers deal with every day is the ever-growing number of new and changing regulations. A recent think tank study analyzed the number of global financial regulations and estimated that over 300 million pages of regulatory documents will be published by 2020.[8] Looking solely at the regulatory guidance for the CRA and the regulation, examiner guidance, Q&As, examination procedures and more add up to over 800 pages of key documents to review, understand and use in a bank's community reinvestment program. That's just to ensure that a CRA program is operating in alignment with best practices and regulatory expectations.

Think about applying that CRA knowledge into practical relationship building in bank markets, and the challenge only increases. As any CRA Officer will tell you, building strong relationships with nonprofit organizations that drive community development is a key component of addressing a community's needs. So, CRA Officers spend time developing these important

[8] Tom Groenfeldt, "Financial Regulations Will Surpass 300 Million Pages by 2020 Says JWG," Fintech – News and Analysis, April 20, 2016, available at https://techandfinance.com/2016/04/20/financial-regulations-will-surpass-300-million-pages-by-2020-says-jwg/

relationships – whether through meetings, luncheons, emails or phone calls.

But what does it mean to build relationships with nonprofits in each and every one of the cities and towns where a bank has a branch? In the United States, there are nearly 1.7 million nonprofits registered with the IRS.[9] This figure excludes many of the government agencies that also support community development. There are also a plethora of online resources that can help a banker identify key data points about nonprofits, many of which use similar data sets in varying ways; but more tools, if not designed or used in the right way, only exacerbate data overload.

To make this a little more tangible, in Nashville, an average Midwest city, there are more than 3,300 registered nonprofits.[10] If a banker spent just five minutes researching each one of these nonprofits online to determine if they were the right CRA partner, it would take him or her nearly seven weeks of full-time work. Which leads me to our last challenge – the resource gap.

THE RESOURCE GAP

In most banks, as in most companies, employees are often asked to work more with less. As a bank's footprint grows and expands with new products, digital offerings and, in some cases, new markets, the same staff members are tasked with stretching their skills and resources to take on these additional developments.
The number of banks in the nation has fallen in the last 10 years, from over 7,000 in 2007 to just fewer than 5,000 today.[11] With this

---

[9] Internal Revenue Service, "Exempt Organizations Business Master File Extract," October 9, 2017, available at https://www.irs.gov/charities-non-profits/exempt-organizations-business-master-file-extract-eo-bmf

[10] Ibid.
[11] Federal Reserve Bank of St. Louis, "Commercial Banks in the U.S.," FRED Economic Data, available at https://fred.stlouisfed.org/series/USNUM

contraction of the players in the market, first through bank failures and now through mergers and acquisitions, bank staff are called on to identify and build new CRA partnerships in markets that are, at best, geographically distant, and in most cases, completely unfamiliar.

So, the solution to the problem of limited resources is finding a way to work smarter in the time we have, which has presented itself in many forms, most underpinned by one commonality – technology.

THE RISE OF REGTECH

Rob Nichols, the current ABA President and CEO, recently said that, "the rapid convergence of banking and technology is a critical issue for the future of the banking industry."[12] This banking and technology convergence has driven the rise of FinTech, and more recently, RegTech. FinTech has changed the way in which consumers access and engage with money. It is meeting consumers where they demand to be met, online and instantly, with new ways to manage and monitor their finances. FinTech is the topic on everyone's minds, analyzed by experts and featured on magazine covers throughout the world.

However, FinTech may be starting to mature. In a recent publication, KPMG provided important analysis regarding U.S. investment trends in FinTech, which once seemed to be on a meteoric rise, growing from $9.1 billion in 2013 to $37.3 billion in 2015. In contrast, as of the first quarter of 2017, only $1.5 billion had been invested into FinTech companies domestically.[13]

---

[12] Rob Nichols, "ABA Fintech > A Commitment to Innovation," ABA Banking Journal, September/October 2017

[13] KPMG, "The Pulse of Fintech Q1 2017: Global Analysis of Investment in Fintech," April 27, 2017, available at https://assets.kpmg.com/content/dam/kpmg/xx/pdf/2017/04/pulse-of-fintech-q1.pdf

If FinTech investment seems to be slowing down, what is the next natural growth in banking technology? Most signs point to RegTech, which is "...the application of technology to help ease banks' regulatory compliance burden."[14] There's no lack of regulatory compliance burden. A recent article from the American Banker estimated that governance, risk and compliance costs reach somewhere between 15 and 20 percent of total "run the bank" costs for most major banks.[15]

RegTech has the potential to shift regulatory compliance in a similar way that FinTech has shifted consumer banking behavior. RegTech is re-thinking and innovating on many of these more straightforward bank data reporting requirements by applying big data and machine learning to empower efficiency in regulatory compliance. However, this type of regulatory compliance is more objective and standardized, which makes it easier to automate. How then can RegTech support the more subjective, relationship-focused world of CRA?

REGTECH AND CRA

From early on, community reinvestment has relied on relationship building – relationships with consumers, borrowers, nonprofits, developers and more. It's about knowing a community, assessing that community's needs and applying targeted support, whether through lending, investment or services, to meet those needs. Since communities are made up of people, this naturally and rightfully is an organic process. The needs that a community had yesterday may be very different next month or next year. A bank's community reinvestment program must adapt to support and empower those needs.

---

[14] Rob Morgan, "The Top Fintech Trends Driving the Next Decade," ABA Banking Journal, September/October 2017, available at https://bankingjournal.aba.com/2017/09/the-top-fintech-trends-driving-the-next-decade/

CRA practitioners are keen experts in identifying their community's needs while also maintaining practical approaches that support a bank's overall goals. They have honed soft skills that allow them to empathize with community partners, analyze potential opportunities and apply complex regulatory requirements in their efforts to ensure a bank's CRA success. In many cases, they are the face of a bank to the people with the most need in a community.

This presents a unique dichotomy – organic, personal community connection versus arms-length, analytical technology. These two choices seem incongruous, at best. One could argue that deploying RegTech to identify and meet CRA requirements will come at the cost of the tangible relationship building that supports the spirit of community reinvestment. I believe the opposite. I am convinced that the power of technology can not only be harnessed, but embraced, to streamline the more analytical parts of CRA and in turn, provide more time and resources to affect greater social impact and measurable change.

There are already solutions available that can support and simplify the research and reinvestment process for banks. These solutions are designed with the needs of CRA professionals in mind, helping to prevent data overload. These new innovators are deploying unique approaches at the intersection of technology and community reinvestment and loosely fall into two groups – the research assistants and the opportunity identifiers.

The research assistants have created online tools that help bankers analyze different parts of the community building process, whether by building performance context, conducting due diligence on nonprofit relationships or measuring their bank's CRA activity. The opportunity identifiers take it a step further. They are organizations that not only help banks build knowledge, but identify and promote specific opportunities for banks to support directly. They simplify community reinvestment by cataloguing lending opportunities, qualifying new investments or promoting specific ways to give back.

Together these innovators are deploying technology as the next step in the evolution of CRA relationship building. It's an area where findCRA is heavily invested as we work to identify every CRA-aligned nonprofit in the United States. We want to make it easy for banks to conduct detailed research and build relationships with those nonprofits in any community through our online platform.

For 40 years, CRA professionals have used their skills to build strong community relationships while simultaneously dealing with the challenges of expanding responsibilities, more community needs and fewer resources. They have made differences in the lives of people and have helped their banks succeed, both in CRA exams and as good corporate citizens. Unfortunately, much of their time is spent analyzing history.

By developing and implementing technology that is designed to support CRA relationship building and research, we can push CRA forward and spend less time researching and more time reinvesting. Purposeful CRA RegTech can empower bankers to make proactive, informed decisions about the relationships they want to build which, in turn, will make a measurable, impactful difference in the communities they serve. I challenge every CRA practitioner to rethink his or her approach to CRA by moving beyond analyzing a bank's history to embracing CRA technology to create its future.

BRIAN WATERS brings over 15 years of experience in regional banking compliance to his role as President and Co-Founder of findCRA, where he focuses on operations and sales as well as driving processes and marketing outreach. During his time in banking, he oversaw regulatory requirements in the area of fair lending, HMDA, CRA, lending, deposit and BSA/AML for a multi-billion dollar regional bank with product offerings in all 50 states. He is a Certified Regulatory Compliance Manager (CRCM), Certified Anti-Money Laundering Professional (AML) and Certified Controls Specialist (CCS). Brian is a graduate of the ABA's National Compliance School and holds Bachelor's of Arts degrees in Business Administration and English from Bellarmine University in Louisville, Kentucky, his hometown.

ABOUT THE EDITOR

Founded in 2013 and headquartered in Louisville, Kentucky, findCRA brings order to the innumerable resources and opportunities available for Community Reinvestment Act participants. The company focuses on educating and qualifying nonprofits to demonstrate their alignment with the federal CRA and on equipping banks with tools and resources to support their relationship building with nonprofits. findCRA offers its services nationally through its Learning Center at www.learnCRA.com and its online platform and Community Qualifier™ search tool at www.findCRA.com.

50505585R00126

Made in the USA
Middletown, DE
31 October 2017